V I C T O R I A   S

The SHADOW WORK JOURNAL

YOUR COMPANION GUIDE TO OUTGROW TRAUMA AND TOXIC PEOPLE
A CBT WORKBOOK FOR ADVANCED SOUL SEARCHERS TO HEAL EMOTIONAL
TRIGGERS, SET BOUNDARIES AND LET YOUR TRUE SELF FREE

WITH CBT INSPIRED WRITING PROMPTS

VOICES OF SUPPORT WORLDWIDE FOR THE SHADOW WORK JOURNAL

I have started my Shadow work journey with Victoria's journal and workbook for beginners. I'm now continuing with this more advanced book of hers, where she is offering her CBT experience to help others exploring very sensitive topics such as how our childhood trauma can impact our adult relationships, and how to increase self awareness to recognise and get out of toxic relationships. The book also offers a very important resource that's a FREE bonus on guilt and shame in the healing process of trauma and a supporting group on FB. What I admire the most about this author is her humanity and openness about the struggles of the human condition. This makes me feel 'normal' in a world of labels and diagnoses. This has made a huge impact in my life. Where before I was feeling lonely and disconnected, I now feel a normal human being in her quest for love and connection.

-AC

This book is a nice guide to help you heal after trauma in your life. Many people suffer from trauma they have experienced as a child, but you have to find a way to heal from the trauma or you will have emotional baggage that is harmful in relationships. Some people suffer from being with a narcissistic person and need to find ways to heal. This book is great in helping anyone get their life back. You need to set boundaries, know your triggers and work through them, accept someone for who they are and move on. I found this book so interesting and helpful.

-Teresa

If you are wanting to delve into those parts of you that need healing this is for you! This explains shadow work in an easy to understand way. The biggest thing is to write about those things that automatically come up that you don't want to write about! It's hard but so worth it! Thank you for this! I'm starting a group with some local women where we can do this together!

-Eli

FREE BONUS

"GUILT AND SHAME AUDIOBOOK"

WHY YOU SHOULD ALSO LISTEN TO THIS AUDIOBOOK BEFORE STARTING READING THE BOOK

1. HOW TO UNDERSTAND THESE EMOTIONS AND HOW TO OVERCOME THEM.

2. BEGIN THE PROCESS OF HEALING TRAUMA AND FORGIVENESS.

At the end of the book (in another bonus section) you will find the QR-Code to scan to get your gift.

We're here
because of you

*If you have found any value in this material,
Please consider leaving a review and joining the Author's
Mission to bring more healing into this world
By scanning the QR-Code below ♥*

★ ★ ★ ★ ★

ALSO BY VICTORIA STEVENS

"BESTSELLER"

Shadow Work Journal and Workbook: The Comprehensive Guide for Beginners to Uncover the Shadow Self & Become Whole as Your Authentic Self | Guided Prompts for Inner Child Soothing, Healing & Growth

SHADOW WORK (BOOK SERIES)

Shadow Work Journal and Workbook for Beginners: Your Companion Guide to Self-Discovery and Self-Love. Recognize The Shadow, Embrace It, And Bring It to Light to Balance Your Life (Book series1)

Shadow Work Journal and Workbook for Beginners: Discover Your Wounded Inner Child and Learn Effective Techniques to Heal It and Reparent It, To Get Over Your Past and Develop Self-Awareness (Book series 2)

Shadow Work Journal and Workbook for Beginners: Your Companion Guide with Interactive Prompts to Integrate the Shadow, Stop Self-Sabotaging Behaviors and Unleash Infinite Creativity (Book series 3)

THE OATH

I, _____ in the face of past adversity and painful sensory experiences lived so far, hereby pledge to resolve what troubles my soul and to recognize, accept, and nurture my wounds.

I vow to be open to guidance and to complete the pages of this journal with commitment and self-compassion, embracing both the conscious and unconscious parts of my being.

I further recognize that living in space and time, as a Creation amongst other Creations, affects my collective destiny. As I heal myself, I heal my family, my community, and I release my ancestors.

I acknowledge to be accountable for my own happiness and fulfilment. As I bring my shadow to light, I bring more light into the world. Love, Joy, Peace and Abundance will manifest as a result.

My legacy to the world is to

So, Be It!

Start Date_____

Signature _____

Completion Date_____

TABLE OF CONTENTS

INTRODUCTION

Have you ever felt trapped? Stuck in your life and experience, like everyone around is moving full steam ahead but you are stagnant. Not going backward, but also not moving forward. Just stuck. Do you feel frustrated with yourself in this stuckness? Like it is your fault that you aren't where you thought you would be, or something must be wrong with you to feel like this.

Most of us will have stuck moments in our lives; it's just a part of life. But trauma has a way of isolating you, of leaving you stuck in that same moment where the world became too big, too scary, and too difficult to deal with. It has a way of trapping you in your past and preventing you from moving forward. It pulls you into the shadows, masking you in the dark to protect you. In the moment, this protection is important—often even vital—but it is time that you let go of your safe space in the cupboard. It's time you stop hiding behind your shadow and step into the light, so that you can truly start to live your life.

Unpacking trauma and confronting your shadow self can be terrifying. I know I was not all too thrilled to begin the journey myself. You have been living with your shadow in control for so long that letting go of it and moving beyond it can feel like losing a part of yourself. It can feel like identity suicide.

But healing from trauma is like planting a seed. There is the parent tree that created the seed, encoded with all the information it will need in its lifetime. The seed will need to find new soil, plant itself, and begin to germinate and grow. The tree that will emerge will be similar to the parent tree in a lot of ways, but it will also be unique and new. It will be stronger and more robust, and it will have gained wisdom on how to survive the wind and the weather.

You are this seed, and at the end of this journey you will emerge new, but the core of who you will remain. You will have new skills to help you roll with the punches and you will not be stuck in that same old soil. You will have found a new path for you to take and you will be able to move forward.

Change is scary, and we are often so incredibly resistant to it...but it is also necessary. This book is here to make this process as easy for you as possible. Rather than you stumbling over internet articles trying to find the information you need to heal, everything is laid out here for you.

This book will use Cognitive-Behavioral Therapy (CBT) inspired work and journaling prompts to help you connect with your shadow self and learn to be kinder to it by establishing an open path of communication. This will also enable you to honestly look at your trauma bonds, emotional triggers, and attachment styles. You will then move onto the healing process by listening to your inner child, which will be done by using the Radical Acceptance approach. You will also learn about how to set boundaries and make healing a daily ritual, as opposed to merely a moment in your life.

The lessons and skills in this book are meant to be lifelong and will provide you with tools and exercises on how to deal with and move through toxic relationships regardless of how close the person is to you and how overwhelming the situation may be. You can work through this book alongside therapy, but it is not necessary, and you can choose to use this book to heal on your own.

Healing is a personal journey. No two traumas are the same and therefore no two healing processes are the same either. The healing process will take work: It will take bravery, it will take resilience and daring. You will stumble, and you might have to take a break, but that is all part of the process, and it is okay. After undergoing six months of Cognitive Behavioral Therapy as a patient, my plan with this book is to provide you with a companion guide for your journey, to pass you tools and also to teach you how to use them, whether you wish to engage in therapy or not. This book is here to help you, to give you information and companionship throughout this process. You are so brave for starting this journey and you are going to make it to a better, happier life.

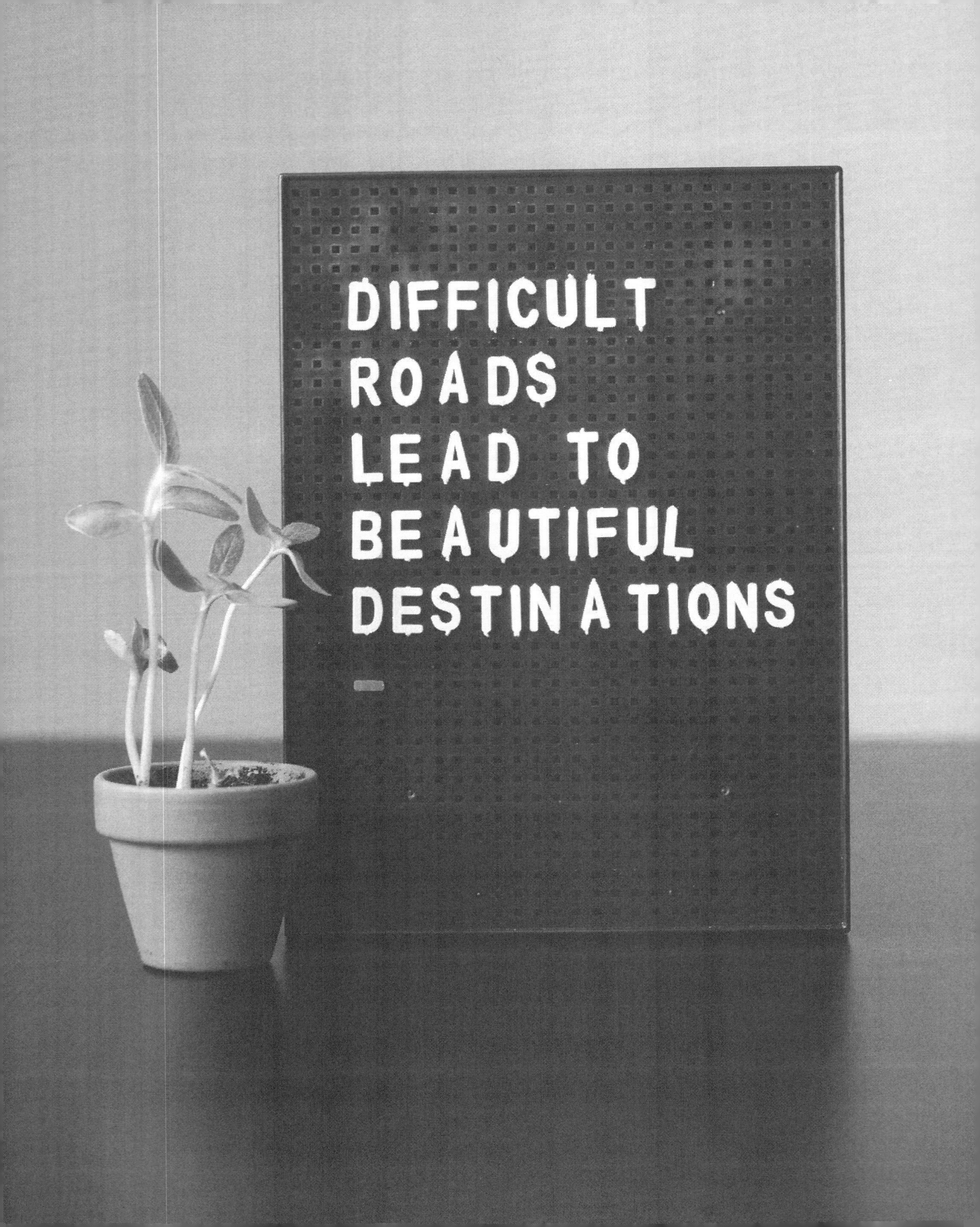
DIFFICULT
ROADS
LEAD TO
BEAUTIFUL
DESTINATIONS

CHAPTER 1:

CHILDHOOD TRAUMA

"We cannot change anything unless we accept it." — Carl Gustav Jung

It's astounding how much influence our childhood can have on our lives. Childhood is a crucial period of development and formation for our future adult lives. Negative situations we find ourselves in as children have the potential to alter the course of our lives. It is not uncommon to suffer psychological effects that change us at a deeper level emotionally. Children soak up everything they see. As a result, while we do not absorb absolutely everything, what we do absorb can stay with us for a very long time.

We are generally unaware of what affects our body, mind, and self-daily. Of course, not all forms of trauma can link to childhood neglect or abuse. Tragedy can manifest in many spheres of our lives. A primary aim of this book is to shed light on how childhood trauma affects everyday life on an emotional level. We want you to feel comfortable exploring your feelings and your sense of self, and understand personal triggers that may affect your life.

Through the use of common psychotherapeutic methods, we will explore this idea. But first, we must remind ourselves that we are not objects to be taken at face value. Instead, we are human beings who need to study more deeply through the Jungian process called "Shadow Work". Simply put, diving deep into your subconscious mind is an active choice. It is a process developed by Swiss psychiatrist Carl Gustav Jung who proposed that our psyches have layers.

But before we can expand upon the concept of Shadow Work and other useful psychotherapeutic methods such as Cognitive Behavioral Therapy, I want to draw your attention back to the complexities of experiencing childhood trauma and what it means.

Because most abuse happens when we are vulnerable, it should be no surprise that it can have a lasting effect on our lives. You see, childhood neglect and abuse can lead to Relational Trauma which tends to have quite a few similarities to PTSD. I want to be careful to not officially diagnose you, the reader of this book, because that is not my job. That being said, I believe that knowledge is the first step to understanding ourselves.

Relational Trauma usually falls into two types: one is Childhood Relational Trauma and the other is Adult Relational Trauma. We are highlighting CRT because I think its topic is more suited to this chapter. As I've said before, caregivers and parents can heavily impact us. I don't think they even realize this, and often we will never get the closure we genuinely want from them. I know I made the mistake of thinking that *only* my parents were responsible for the childhood trauma I suffered.

In many cases, I dealt with other authority figures who had something to say about how I was growing up, and it was rarely positive. If I can be transparent for a small moment, I don't think it's easy to admit that we need help. We look at others and want to be like them, but we should embrace what makes us ourselves. Often CRT can be a source of our lack of trust, insecurities, and unstable relationships and can be tied to numerous factors. These factors are childhood abuse, neglect, and inconsistent parenting. Suffering constant bullying can have a similar impact. Most of the time, it's what we experience at the hands of caregivers. CRT can complicate aspects of your life you might not be immediately aware of and cause adverse effects such as feeling insecure in what should be a secure relationship.

Although I was lucky enough to recognize trauma that originated from my childhood and due to my parents, many others are not so lucky. Parents are human as well, and make mistakes, some of which are a result of their own trauma. It is often hard to recognize that your parents may have been abusive or neglectful because it was done in such a way that it seemed almost normal.

This is especially more difficult if you are not an only child. When your siblings don't share your trauma or feelings, it makes it easier to say that it couldn't have been as a result of your parents because you had the same ones. It also makes it more difficult to explore your trauma openly. As I said in the introduction, trauma is not something that happens *to* us, but instead something that happens *inside* us.

Every person thinks, feels and processes differently. This means that if you had a parent that had severe anxiety, for example, your siblings would think about it in a different way than you, it would make them feel differently and they would process it completely differently. When your siblings see your parent have an anxiety attack and are completely unphased, it could affect your sense of security and understanding of the event, which will cause you trauma but not them. If at a young age you presented yourself as more responsible, your parents might have become more codependent on you. This does not always have to be in regards to you taking on responsibility over your siblings, but perhaps even responsibility over the feelings of your parents. When they argued, you would be made a part of it; when they were stressed over something, they shared this burden with you, a child who was not supposed to carry this burden.

I would like to emphasize to you that people with the highest awareness and the most enlightened people tend all to have highly traumatic experiences in their past. Therefore, trauma should be taken also as an opportunity to increase awareness and spirituality. Here I'd like to mention to you that people that can be seen as the gurus of the self-help industry (such as Louise Hay, Wayne Dyer and many others that have literally helped millions of people around the world) all had major issues in their childhood and adulthood.

"The greatest damage done by neglect, trauma or emotional loss is not the immediate pain they inflict but the long-term distortions they induce in the way a developing child will continue to interpret the world and her situation in it. All too often these ill-conditioned implicit beliefs become self-fulfilling prophecies in our lives. We create meanings from our unconscious interpretation of early events, and then we forge our present experiences from the meaning we've created. Unwittingly, we write the story of our future from narratives based on the past."

— Dr. Gabor Maté, In the Realm of Hungry Ghosts: Close Encounters with Addiction

Affirmation: I must focus on my journey and who I am in this present day. It is here for me to be my most authentic self.

Using the following writing prompt, I want you to take a moment to uncover the essence of yourself and who you think you are, based on the experiences you might have had as a child. That way you can outline the most apparent struggles you might have when thinking of past experiences. Remember, there is no wrong answer, and you can use these pages to reference back to them as we start to unpack the effects of childhood trauma throughout these sections.

- [ ] What is your earliest childhood memory (good or bad)?
- [ ] What is the one part of yourself you wish you could change?
- [ ] What five things do you think are the most important to you?
- [ ] What is something you would tell your younger self?
- [ ] What did you love to do as a child?
- [ ] What did you hate to do as a child?
- [ ] How would you define love? (It doesn't have to be romantic.)
- [ ] What would you do if you could do something without fail?
- [ ] Name one thing you are proud of from your past. What about it would you share with someone?
- [ ] Write a summary of a person you admire and what they mean to you.

WRITING PROMPT: REFLECTION

WRITING PROMPT: REFLECTION

JOURNAL PROMPT: THE FIRST STEP

The next page is your first journal prompt. These will be here to write down your thoughts without any restrictions. This exercise is about unlocking that inner reflection muscle needed to free yourself from the oppressive and intrusive thoughts plaguing your mind. As you can see, this one is named the "First Step". I want you to reflect upon the things you feel are the most pressing in your life and which of these are perhaps a result of your childhood.

THE FIRST STEP

ATTACHMENT STYLES

"Loyalty to that which does not work, or worse, to a person who is toxic, exploitive or destructive to you, is a form of insanity." — Patrick J. Carnes

As I previously stated, trauma can come in many shapes and sizes, but the focus here is what childhood trauma can mean to us.

I'm sure your first reaction to the phrase childhood trauma is usually the extreme cases. But I want to unpack this by saying that negative childhood experiences take many forms. Often, the care you received as a child will impact your external behaviors in relationships. Something as small as a caregiver continually withholding physical affection can cause confusing behaviors. One behavior is to keep others at a distance and be suspicious of physical interaction. Then there's being borderline clingy due to your lack of affection as a child. It is easy to see how our guardians' actions affect us and will almost always impact how we end up in our adult lives.

Before I get ahead of myself and overwhelm you with information, I want to ensure that you are still considering your own state of mind. If, at any point in this book, the topics become too heavy, do not feel ashamed if you can't deal with a topic at the moment. We are all human, and the goal of this book is to help you understand yourself, to encourage you to give yourself the space to explore the person beneath the layers. Something I've learned in researching this topic is that the reason we are built the way we are is that, at some point, we have put up boundaries to protect ourselves. It's not always immediately negative. Think of it as a way for our inner selves to protect us. Most of the time, we'll find a good reason why we started behaving as we did.

So what am I getting at here? Well, I want to bring your attention to the concept of attachment styles. Four major attachment styles tend to form based on our relationships with our guardians. They are as follows:

- **Anxious:** This style can come across as 'clingy' or 'needy' and tends to ultimately rely on the responses people receive from their partners. They essentially want to hold on as tight as possible to their relationships to prevent them from falling apart. Every time someone pulls away from an anxious attachment style person, they tend to become desperate to keep and maintain that relationship.

- **Avoidant:** This style can also be referred to as the 'Dismissive' attachment style. These people consider themselves independent and, on an emotional level, overly confident. While they might not have problems with physical affection, they tend to avoid emotional closeness and would prefer never to depend on anyone.

- **Disorganized:** This is the rarest of the attachment styles and a highly complex one. Essentially a person with this style wants closeness with the people around them, but at the same time, they have intense trouble with trusting people and tend to flip-flop between avoidant and anxious. One of the biggest problems is emotion regulation since most of their actions are generated via fear of getting hurt.

- **Secure:** All the other three attachment styles discussed are based on insecurities that arise in a person due to their childhood nurturing. The secure style is the healthiest and is usually based on the person being confident in themself and the people around them. These are people that can balance their lifestyles with those in their lives. They have strong boundaries and don't become overly dependent on people, but can still trust them.

The importance of looking into our attachment style is that it points to the origin of our trauma, especially when these are from our childhood. It also helps us to see when we ourselves are acting in unhealthy ways, as well as allows us to identify the emotional triggers that we have developed due to this childhood trauma. Identifying our attachment style may also help us to see why we are attracted to toxic relationships and abusive environments. These can act like an early identification system for us to avoid future trauma.

I want you to use this prompt to go over your interaction with the people in your life. Whether this is a romantic partner or a coworker, it doesn't matter as the focus of this exercise is to help you understand how you interact with those around you. It's also important to remember that you won't fit into every attachment style perfectly and to never 'diagnose' yourself with anything if you haven't consulted a professional. I encourage independent research, and I want people to be able to stand on their own two feet, but humans always need support.

- Who do you value the most in your life?

- If you could give someone in your life a gift, what would that gift be?

- What is the most important aspect for you in a relationship?

- What are the qualities of your caregiver that you dislike?

- List three people in your life that you struggle to connect with, and then list a quality about them that you love.

- Who would you spend it with if you had one day left to live?

- What is your fondest memory of being appreciated, and what was the circumstance surrounding it?

- What is a dealbreaker in your relationships with people?

- ☐ Do you enjoy spending time with people? What are your favorite activities to do?

- ☐ Are you comfortable with your current life balance?

WRITING PROMPT: RELATIONSHIPS

JOURNAL PROMPT: CHILDHOOD

In this prompt I want you to write down two passages.

One is the childhood you actually had: Write down how you grew up, who was present, who was not, including those that caused trauma. You could include a memory or scenario that describes your childhood perfectly.

In the second passage, I want you to create your ideal childhood. What could have been different, who would have been absent and who would be present? Make up a scenario or change a memory to become perfect.

CHILDHOOD

Affirmation: By loving myself, I can learn to love others and be open to other experiences in my life.

EMOTIONAL TRIGGERS

"Man's task is to become conscious of the contents that press upward from the unconscious." — Carl Gustav Jung

I've talked a lot about self-love and identifying insecurities in your relationships.

I wanted now to take a moment to touch on something I've brought up once or twice, which is the concept of taking care of yourself. In this section, I want to elaborate on what I meant by becoming aware of your limits. Later, we will look into concepts such as setting boundaries and how to identify when you are in a toxic relationship with someone. This is the section where I want you to focus on yourself because, while external awareness is essential, it is nowhere near as important to me as ensuring that you are taking care of yourself. I know that's something that took me years to learn. I spent so much of my healing journey trying to take other people into account that I ended up leaving myself behind. Your mental health is just as important as that of those around you.

In recent times people have diminished the meaning of triggers. Most people believe being 'triggered' is someone being 'overdramatic' or conflating a minor occurrence in their life to get across the seriousness of a situation they are in. But being triggered is a very real experience, and we should always listen to the needs of our bodies. It takes time to learn, and a book like this should never be a replacement for professional help, but I hope that through this chapter, I can give you a little understanding of what awaits you when you take on this journey of introspection. See it as testing the waters but not throwing you into the deep end.

So, what is a trigger, or in this case, an emotional trigger? Simply put, it is when a previous event causes you to have an intense, almost unnatural response to something that is currently happening. It sends you back to the original negative experience. I can speak from a personal viewpoint here due to my upbringing. When I was younger, my parents reacted to every little thing they deemed incorrect, which ended in verbal screaming matches between my father and me. I was so young that my awareness of whatever happened was minuscule. This didn't stop him from tearing down my self-worth and labeling me useless and incapable of finishing even the smallest of tasks. In his eyes, I could never do right. This is why in my adulthood, I get riddled with anxiety whenever I make what I perceive as a mistake. When I feel my side of a story is not heard, I start to get irrationally angry and cry uncontrollably. My emotions begin to control me, and I feel as if all I want to do is sink into a dark hole where no one can find me again. I'm sure you have all been there; it is almost as if you revert to an infantile state.

This type of behavior isn't inherently wrong, but it often gets labeled as such to shame people into submission. This is why I want to bring up the fact that seeking therapy is vital. My preferred therapy form is CBT (Cognitive Behavioral Therapy). It's a process of flipping the way you perceive and interpret your emotions and mental health issues into a more constructive light. Learning my emotional triggers took a lot of work, and now that I am older, it seems so much easier to identify what is holding me back from functioning throughout my days. I'll elaborate on CBT soon; I just want to first bring the conversation back to our emotional triggers, as for each person, they are different.

I do find, however, that there are a general number of categories that our symptoms tend to fall into. Someone once explained that when we are faced with our emotional responses, it is not because we are horrible people but because our bodies and minds have become hotwired to protect us. The people around us, regardless of their intentions, tend to back us up into corners unknowingly, and we become desperate to claw ourselves free. It is hard to swallow that you won't always have the same solutions to problems that an average person already comes equipped with, but you don't have to despair because the secret is that we are never alone. As you go through this book, I hope it gives you the sense of comfort I needed when I was younger.

Here are some of the symptoms you might experience if you have been faced with emotionally stressful situations:

☐ Rapid breathing

☐ Intense anxiety that can lead to panic attacks

☐ Uncontrollable crying

☐ Irrational anger, or just general anger

☐ Light-headedness

☐ Nausea, constipation, or overall, physically feeling unwell

☐ Trembling, a sense of doom

☐ Chest pain, rapid heart rate, and flushed cheeks

These are not the only symptoms, but they are the most common. Essentially, your body acts to get you out of the situation and environment as fast as possible. I like to compare it to the fight or flight response. We all have this—again, it is a form of survival in a dangerous world. So, let's say a car is hurtling your way, and you only have seconds to act. Most of the time, you will probably be paralyzed and ready to take on the car or jump out of the way. Emotional triggers are when that instinct has been activated an unhealthy amount of times. With my relationship with my parents, I was always walking on eggshells waiting for that car to plow me down. There was no moment of peace in my mind. I had to either flee or fight, and choosing to fight was never a good idea. You can't be blamed for how you react if that is all you know.

I'm here to help you change that.

With this writing prompt, I want to emphasize your ability to handle certain scenarios. Whether you are bad or good at them doesn't matter as this is just about you understanding your emotions and starting to identify them without the pressure of having to confront every single one.

- ❏ Make a list of five emotions that you are likely to feel (anything from love to anger), and write them down from most important to least important.

- ❏ Pick one emotion you think is positive, and write down your reason why.

- ❏ Pick one emotion you see as negative, and write down why.

- ❏ Do you have emotional triggers? Write them down and reflect on them.

- ❏ What is a way you have figured out on your own to deal with your emotional triggers?

- ❏ What is one emotion you are constantly trying to hide?

- ❏ Why do you hide this emotion? Is there something about it that scares you?

- ❏ What do you think this emotion protects you from?

- ❏ What makes you feel that you can't face this emotion?

- ❏ Think of one moment in your past that might be the source of this emotion. There's no right or wrong answer, but I want you to just reflect on this.

WRITING PROMPT: IDENTIFICATION

Writing Prompt: Identification

Journal Prompt: Discovery

We can often be quite hard on ourselves and tend not to take the time to reflect on our internal emotions. In this prompt, I want you just to write—take emotions that can be negative or positive, and just write. What I mean is for you to uncover every corner of these emotions and try to understand the reason for their existence.

I like to paint a mental picture of my emotions and write a little story. It's a bit out there, but I'm willing to share it to help you feel more comfortable and realize that this book is a judgment-free zone. I like to say my emotions are a group of people sitting around a conference table discussing my well-being and their job is to help me get through a situation. Anger is what fights my injustice; sadness reminds me I am still human; and happiness is the light that flickers when I need to be reminded that there is beauty in the smallest of things. Of course, this is an oversimplification of the complexities of my multi-faceted psyche, but I hope you get the idea.

Let your creativity, or whichever way you express yourself, flow on the pages.

DISCOVERY

IS THIS MY TRAUMA OR MY PARENTS TRAUMA?

"It takes enormous trust and courage to allow yourself to remember." — Bessel A. van der Kolk

As I've mentioned, the trauma experienced in childhood can be a result of your parents' trauma. So how do we differentiate between when we are reacting to our own trauma or that of our parents?

I would like to use another example here. Let's say you have a parent that is extremely scared of large bodies of water. This trauma comes from when they were a child and saw somebody drown. This is completely normal and to be expected, but now whenever they see their children in a pool, lake or ocean, they get extremely anxious to the point of a panic attack. As a result, their children never learned how to swim and have never spent any time in a body of water. Now as adults, these children go on holiday to the beach. When they arrive there, they are completely comfortable relaxing on the beach, but refuse to get into the water, because they cannot swim and are scared of being swept in by the current.

Is this still their parents' trauma or has this now become theirs?

The easy answer here is that this is still their parents' trauma, simply because this person can still learn to swim and will become more comfortable with larger bodies of water, without actually requiring a large amount of therapy, whereas if it were their own trauma, they would need major therapy for this and even then may not ever be comfortable in the situation.

It is important that you take a long and hard look at your trauma and identify where it comes from, whether it belongs to you or to someone that influenced your life. Examples of these would be like being scared of large crowds, because this usually triggered a parent's anxiety, or having an aversion towards alcohol because your parents grew up with alcoholic parents or siblings and as a result banned and villainized alcohol.

To identify your own trauma, see if you can connect this trauma to a specific event that happened to *you*—but be warned, especially when it comes to trauma, your brain may have locked that event away and you may need help unlocking the memory to know about it and understand it.

NON-ABUSIVE OR NEGLECTFUL PARENTS

"About a third of my cases are suffering from no clinically definable neurosis, but from the senselessness and emptiness of their lives. This can be defined as the general neurosis of our times." — Carl Gustav Jung

I've been addressing CRT by focusing on how to deal with it when it was caused by your parents, but there is a large number of people who have suffered from relational trauma that was not caused by their parents. So what do we do in a situation like this? Well, the first step would be to identify where it came from. This could be from toxic siblings, school bullies, or even other toxic authority figures like nannies, teachers, neighbors and more.

You will often find that most of your relational trauma would have been caused by the same person, so when you think back on your trauma, who is the person that comes to your mind most often?

This is normally a person that was influential in our lives for a long period of time, so you should be able to recall at least a few circumstances where this person may have made you feel drained, negative and uncomfortable.

I would like to remind you that sometimes emotionally unavailable parents and self-absorbed parents can create trauma without being materially neglectful. Some people are raised in opulence but lack the emotional connections needed to develop into fulfilled adults. They feel they have been housed and fed, but equally, they feel they have never been heard.

Once you have identified this person it is easier to identify more of the trauma they have caused you and to work through it. It is also important to note that trauma can be caused by more than one person. You may have trauma stemming from a variety of interactions and a variety of people. This should not make you feel bad—however, it is a sign that you are an empath. You more easily take on the emotions of others and they find it easier to influence you. This also does not make you weak—remember that you were a child, trusting those around you to nourish and protect you. It is not your responsibility as a child to be an adult.

HOW DO I LET GO?

"If you are going to go to the trouble of choosing healthy food for your plate, shouldn't you also choose healthy people for your life?" — Ramani Durvasula

You have already taken the first steps towards letting go—by reading this book you've already begun accepting that you need to heal. We'll be covering more direct ways to help you let go of your trauma and the ongoing emotional triggers that are used to trap you in a toxic relationship, but there are indirect ways to help yourself as well.

We need to look at both conscious and subconscious efforts, and while therapy and the exercises in this book are all conscious efforts, I would like to add some ideas and techniques for subconscious efforts as well.

The main cause of our trauma and ongoing emotional triggers is the fact that these emotions have been trapped within us for so long that we have gotten so used to them, and we think of them as a part of ourselves. While we will actively be focusing on getting these emotions out, understanding them and working with them will help us in the long-run. Nevertheless, this can get very exhausting in the short-term as it is constant work.

Luckily there are ways to get your emotions out without working on them directly. Activities that are seen as fun and recreational can help us with this. Have you ever listened to a song or musical composition that actually made your chest feel heavy and your eyes wet even though it was beautiful? This is when those that created it actually poured their feelings into it and used this piece of creativity to let their emotions out and help them to be rid of their own trauma.

You, however, do not need to sing or play an instrument. You can use other activities like writing. Even if you never publish a book, just write for yourself. Or you can try painting. Again you don't ever have to sell a painting, just take the brush and canvas, and free your emotions.

So what about those that aren't as artistically inclined, or have no interest in this? You can use other activities such as yoga as a way to get your emotions out.

The main focus here is to engage in something that affords you a break from the world, but still allows you to express your emotions. When doing these activities, you are focusing your mind and relaxing your body, releasing the physical tension as well as emotional tension at the same time.

Affirmation: I've managed to survive all this while in the dark. Now that I have the answers, I can find my way out.

In this prompt I want you to look into the origins of your relational trauma and where it came from. The purpose of this is to help you self-reflect on trauma and sort through it.

- [ ] What trauma of other people are you holding on to?

- [ ] How can you let go of trauma from others?

- [ ] What trauma of your own are you holding on to?

- [ ] Where does your own trauma stem from?

- [ ] How can you let go of your own trauma?

- [ ] What activity do you feel will best let you subconsciously let out your emotions?

- [ ] Who was the biggest influence on your childhood relational trauma?

WRITING PROMPT: ORIGINS

Journal Prompt: A Love Letter to Myself

In this section, I want you to sit down and write a letter to yourself. Don't be afraid to dive into your insecurities, as they are a part of you and important to look into. You should reflect on the most traumatic events and people of your past and present, how they may have affected your personality and shaped your attachment style in the present moment, and how you would like to see yourself in the near future. Look at 5 to 10 years forward in time. Which emotional triggers do you want to tackle and which emotion do you want to soothe? Then look at if you still see the same people around. Do you still enjoy the same lifestyle? If not, what do you want to see happening in your future?

A LOVE LETTER TO MYSELF

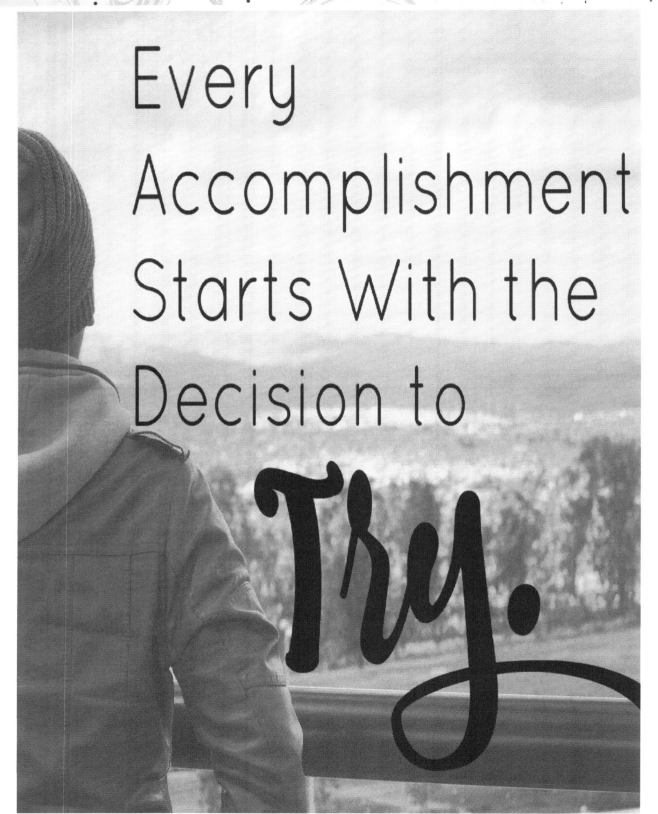

Every Accomplishment Starts With the Decision to Try.

CHAPTER 2:

HEALTHY COPING

MECHANISMS

"Acceptance is the only way out of hell." — Marsha M. Linehan

Calling something a "coping mechanism" has quite the implication, doesn't it? I have found that when people use this phrase, it's almost in a nonchalant fashion. Phrases like "I like shopping, it's my coping mechanism" come to mind. However, there is a deeper meaning to it than just accepting the phrases at face value, and, as you can tell, I am all about peeling back the layers and discovering that hidden, more profound personal truth.

Almost everyone has coping mechanisms; sometimes, we aren't even aware of them. Often, those coping mechanisms are formed subconsciously, and can be created due to several factors. This isn't to say we don't make deliberate choices to cope with certain aspects of our lives. It means it's not as simple as people want you to believe. Coping mechanisms are strategies we use to process stressful situations and trauma we might have experienced. So just like we covered emotional triggers, a coping mechanism can be the tool we use to try to appease that trigger when we can. Think of it as a way for our brains to adjust to a situation we are uncomfortable with in any way, shape, or form. Shame should not weigh down our triggers and coping mechanisms because they are our inner self crying out and acknowledging that the pain we are feeling is there and is real. At the end of it, coping mechanisms are also the way we can work through and process our days.

Something else to consider is that coping mechanisms have many facets. There isn't just one type of coping mechanism but numerous. We've got relaxation, compulsion, escapism, and even things such as problem-solving. On the surface level, this might not sound so bad—after all, what are the adverse effects of taking a little time for yourself and de-stressing from life? But, unfortunately, I think that is where many of us fall into a trap. Harmless coping mechanisms can easily turn into unhealthy habits. Perhaps you are the sort of person to exercise as a way to get rid of all the pent emotions that threaten to bubble over, and, don't get me wrong, the benefits of exercise are vast. But too much of it, as with anything in excess, can cause serious health issues and often overexertion. Are you an artist? Do you thrive on the next big piece that will give you the emotional clarity you crave? Then you need to look out for burnout, which is almost along the same lines as overexertion but is more on a mental basis.

Of course, we can also develop defense mechanisms too; they aren't too far apart from our coping habits, but they are usually the ones we form on a subconscious level. For example, you will find quite a few people use things such as humor to deflect from any conversation that requires any form of introspection. They might even take part in escapist behavior like going to an excessive amount of social events or even wholly shutting themselves away from the world by playing video games. Neither one is any less significant. It all depends on the views of society.

I feel it important here that we note that each and every person will have different ways of coping: We will have different triggers, and different reactions to our triggers. This is perfectly valid. Nobody can tell you that your feelings and reactions are invalid or wrong, and it is imperative that we focus on what triggers us and how we can respond to it. When we get attuned to these emotions, we allow ourselves to validate the emotions of not only our inner child but also the emotions of those around us.

Many of our triggers and reactions to them are directly connected to ACE's (Adverse Child Experiences). These can lead to unhealthy coping mechanisms such as substance abuse, and ACE's have also been linked to causing a negative impact on the development of a child's brain. This can cause a variety of problems in adults ranging from learning disabilities to, in quite severe cases, mental illness such as Dissociative Identity Disorder. It goes without saying that these disorders and illnesses should be treated by a professional, and we will be focusing on assisting with treatment of less severe disorders. It is however still important to note these uncomfortable truths so we can fully understand our emotions.

There are a great deal of studies and other books that I have found extremely valuable in researching and understanding ACE's and their connections to our adult lives. You will notice that I've incorporated them here.

I mention ACE's here instead of under the previous chapter because I would like to point out that they could be very different from relational trauma. ACE's tend to more directly affect emotional triggers than relational trauma.

When it comes to emotional triggers, one of the experts I have found most helpful, Dr Gabor Maté, teaches that being triggered involves two people. Being triggered is your emotional response to the actions of an outside influence, but, through hard work and proper healing, we can change our responses to triggers to be a lot more healthy. This would be our healthy coping mechanism.

Before we move on, I would like to leave you with a quote from Dr. Maté:

We shouldn't be ashamed of it because it's just an acknowledgement that we've suffered pain... Triggers are great to work with. Get to know yourself. You are the one with explosives inside you. Defuse it by getting to know yourself, aware of yourself...somebody pulled that trigger but who's carrying that ammunition and how you handle people that trigger you, that's your call but at least know that you're the one with all the ammunition, and you're the one with all the explosives inside you. And you'll get so much liberation through getting to know yourself, that's where freedom lies, that nobody had the power to trigger you, not because you're shut down or numb or isolated, but because you are totally aware of yourself, that's where liberation actually is.

Victoria Stevens
THE BENEFITS OF SHADOW WORK

"Who looks outside, dreams; who looks inside, awakes." — Carl Gustav Jung

I hope I've established by now that it's OK to get triggered and employ some kind of coping mechanism afterward. But how do you start to take a step in the direction of self-help and move towards actualizing your true self?

I want to highlight a fantastic psychotherapy method pioneered by Carl Jung called "Shadow Work". I briefly discussed it in the previous chapter. Shadow Work connects with what Jung refers to as our "Inner Child" and our "Shadow". The Inner Child is that person deep inside you that embodies the joy and light you feel. It is sometimes vulnerable and scared but, like any other child, it can be helped to feel safe and secure again.

By helping our inner child to heal from our past trauma and experiences, we can help ourselves to also start feeling happy and secure again, and once we have done that, our traumas cannot be used as a familiarity to lull us back into a false sense of security. This is in essence what narcissists do during the trauma bonding of relationships that we will look at a bit later on.

Shadow Work can be used to help you develop healthy coping mechanisms while working through past trauma. It will also help you to break free from that trauma so it no longer defines you.

When we do Shadow Work we interact with what Dr. Jung defined as our "Inner Shadow", the parts of us that we subconsciously reject. These parts of ourselves directly tie in to ACE's and relational trauma; for example, if you grew up being told that you speak way too much, your parents constantly reprimanded you about it, or you were teased about it at school, you eventually start to believe that it is true and that it is a negative part of your personality. As an adult, this then becomes a part of your Shadow Self, and without you realizing it, you will constantly be making an effort to make sure you don't talk too much, whether in verbal conversation or in other mediums such as texting or sending professional emails. The problem comes in when you don't address your Shadow Self, and these aspects of your personality become emotional triggers due to the fact that you are constantly diverting focus to these aspects, and often over-analyzing them. You tend to already have a negative feeling towards them, and when someone brings these traits up or points them out, you get triggered. Let's say, for example, you go out with a friend and they introduce you to someone they know, you will be nervous, you will try and be on your best behavior, and you will be especially self-critical over the traits of your Shadow Self. If you then afterwards get told something along the lines of "Wow, you were very talkative," it will immediately trigger those negative feelings inside of you, and you will feel extremely offended by this otherwise innocent comment. This is due to the fact that you invested so much of yourself into not being too talkative that it hurts you, and most of the time you won't understand why.

This is where Shadow Work comes in, and will help you to uncover aspects of your Shadow Self and to eventually accept it as part of yourself. By accepting it, you can deal with these traits in a healthy way, which will minimize negative emotional reactions while also leading to greater self-acceptance. We will then further heal by using journaling and writing prompts that are heavily influenced by CBT. These prompts will help you to identify your negative thoughts and shape them into more positive thoughts through the power of your own pen.

So how does this tie in with our relationships and breaking the cycle of trauma bonding and the hold that narcissists have over us? Well, we'll get into that in more detail a bit later on, but, essentially, when you are aware and in touch with your shadow self, a narcissist cannot use that to break you down, and this will help you break away from their control. At the same time if you have already survived a narcissist and are trying to heal, Shadow Work will show you that the narcissist has been breaking you down and that you are nowhere near as unlovable and broken as a narcissist tries to convince you that you are. This will help you to see your real value, to see what you are actually worth, and to rebuild yourself and heal the wounds this person left on you.

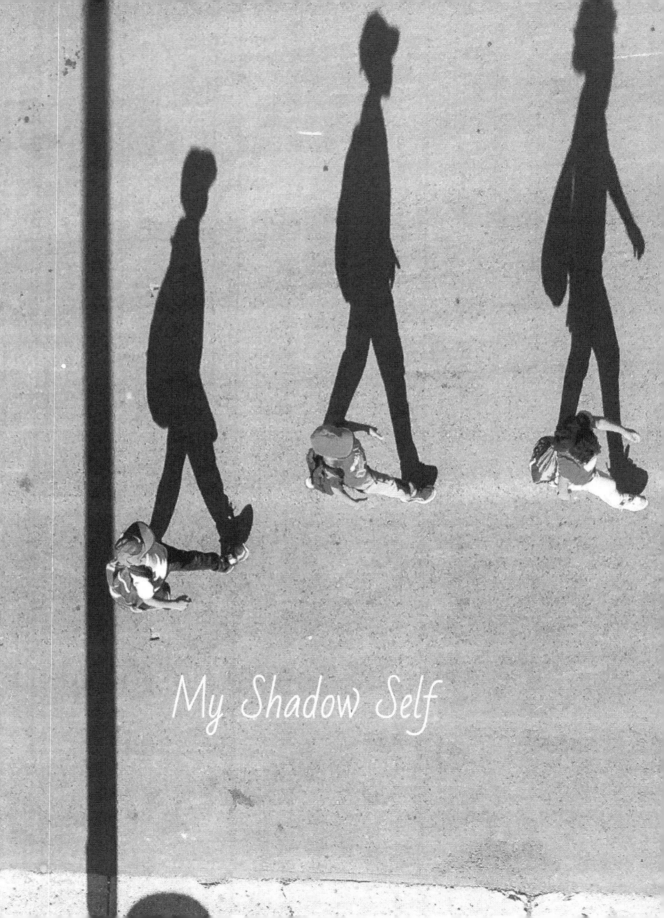

My Shadow Self

In this prompt I want you to explore your inner child. What makes this aspect of your personality happy and what value does it add to your life? These are the emotions that give you the most child-like reactions to your emotions, good and bad, for example, when you start snort laughing uncontrollably, or when you get so angry you clench your fists, frown at something and just yell incoherently.

- [ ] What are a few of your wants inspired by your inner child? This can be anything like a gaming system, a bubblegum milkshake once in a while, things that you don't actually need or would normally want in your day-to-day life, but that actually make your inner child happy.

- [ ] Which emotion do you feel is most connected to your inner child and why? For example, you could say jealousy, because no matter what your sister does wrong, she always got a reward, so you started to become jealous of the attention and materialistic things she got that you didn't.

- [ ] What emotion would you say is most disconnected from your inner child and why? For example, you could say sadness, because as a child whenever you were sad, you were given something that would make you stop being sad, so your inner child still doesn't understand what sadness is.

- [ ] What value does your inner child add to your life?

- [ ] What aspect of your life is made more difficult by your inner child?

- [ ] How connected do you feel to your inner child?

- [ ] How often do you feel at odds with your inner child?

- [ ] What is the greatest lesson taught to you by your inner child recently?

WRITING PROMPT: MY SHADOW SELF

Journal Prompt: Trauma

Look at the word 'trauma'. What does it mean to you? How can you relate to it? Write down a passage that not only helps you to explain trauma, but also relational trauma. Use personal experiences as examples.

TRAUMA

WHAT IS CBT?

"So self-acceptance does not mean self-admiration or even self-liking at every moment of our lives, but tolerance for all our emotions, including those that make us feel uncomfortable." — Gabor Maté

A common result from both ignoring your Shadow Self and being in a toxic relationship is that you suffer from anxiety and depression. This is caused when you reject the parts of you that make up your Shadow Self, and is aggravated when these parts are made to seem even worse than they actually are during trauma bonding experiences. One of the most popular ways of dealing with this and repairing the damage to you is through the use of Cognitive Behavioral Therapy, or as we'll refer to it, CBT.

When someone suffers from something like anxiety or depression, they get stuck in this negative thought loop. They already feel bad about themselves, their self-esteem is very low and their thoughts are dark. These dark thoughts tend to pop up quite often and allow negative comments about a person to break them down even further. This puts them in an even darker place, a place where the negative thoughts are much louder. This is where CBT comes in.

Through this therapeutic treatment the negative thoughts are identified, then challenged to prove them wrong, before finally being replaced with thoughts that are more objective and realistic. This allows CBT to tie in with Shadow Work quite a bit as it forces you to look at your Shadow Self and then change your perspective on it, as well as change your Shadow Self's perspective on you.

This is achieved through several different methods. The first of which is Cognitive Therapy. This is the technique where the negative thinking patterns, behaviors and even emotional responses are identified and changed for the better. These negative aspects are usually those that make up your Shadow Self, and, since Shadow Work is about accepting and working with these parts of you, this will help you to promote acceptance and learn how to use these aspects of you as a way to improve and build yourself up, instead of breaking yourself down.

Another technique is Dialectical Behavior Therapy, or DBT for short. This technique looks at the thoughts and behaviors that cause these negative thought patterns and uses strategies such as emotional regulation to help the person to completely control their emotional state and improve it to fight this darkness. A very important and useful aspect to this is radical acceptance, a technique we will be looking into in greater detail in just a moment.

The next technique is called Multimodal Therapy. This approach suggests that certain psychological issues need to be treated. This is done through addressing seven different interconnected modalities. They are: behavior, affect, sensation, imagery, cognition, interpersonal factors, and drug/biological considerations. This allows us to address our good and bad at the same time—the entire us, our conscious self and our shadow self. This can help to create a bridge between the two and allow us to address several issues at the same time, like for example addressing childhood trauma and how it impacts us as adults, while also looking at the wounds a recent toxic relationship inflicted on us and the connection between them.

The last treatment involved in CBT is Rational Emotive Behavior Therapy, or REBT for short. This involves identifying irrational beliefs and then actively challenging these beliefs before finally learning how to recognize and change these thought patterns. This technique can be used to help us make our Shadow Self nicer to us, and to look at the world around us in a better light. When we look around us and think negative thoughts, this is a technique we can use to change that negativity, challenge it and look at it from a different viewpoint.

As you can see, CBT is a great tool that I really think can help someone to break away from the emotional triggers left behind by past trauma. This is why it is often used during therapy to help victims of narcissistic abuse and especially in conjunction with Shadow Work.

Where Shadow Work allows you to find the repressed part of yourself, the parts that you normally do not like and the parts that normally get broken down, CBT helps you change the narrative about yourself when you are thinking about these parts, but also extends further and helps to change your narrative about yourself as a whole.

When you hear those intrusive thoughts that tell you that you talk too much, CBT can be used to change those thoughts into something positive and constructive. These intrusive thoughts are also often a result of relational trauma and will most often reflect negative criticism you heard while growing up.

When our thoughts are constantly breaking us down, they can lead to depression and anxiety. In this prompt I want you to look at these negative thoughts and emotional responses and consider how you can change them. Create an action plan that you can implement in your daily life.

- ☐ What are the thoughts that break you down the most?
- ☐ How can you change these thoughts into something more positive?
- ☐ Where do these thoughts come from?
- ☐ What are situations in which you have found yourself reacting negatively
- ☐ How can you change these reactions to be more positive?
- ☐ Why do you react negatively during these situations?

WRITING PROMPT: CHANGE

Journal Prompt: Positive Reinforcement

In this prompt I want you to make up affirmations and mantras that you can use to help build yourself up whenever you feel depressed and down. Focus especially on the thoughts you have identified that break you down the most. These affirmations and mantras should be something you can wake up and say to yourself and read every morning that will give you the energy and the will to face the day.

POSITIVE REINFORCEMENT

Victoria Stevens
RADICAL ACCEPTANCE

"What you resist, persists." — Neale Donald Walsch

Often when someone hears the term and the definition of radical acceptance they believe that it means you should just give up. I would like to start this section by telling you that this is nothing more than a common misconception.

To put it simply for you, radical acceptance means that you accept that something negative happened to you. You do not need to accept what happened, why or how, but simply that it did happen and that it happened to you. This is often a large part of where we get stuck in our healing phase, with questions like "Why me?" We are always wondering why we had the bad parents, why we had to meet the narcissist, why we had to get in the accident—but as soon as we start accepting that it has happened and that we cannot change the facts, we can finally allow ourselves to begin healing.

Unfortunately, we will not always have the answer as to why these things happen to us, whether it's luck of the draw, or a case that we just don't see the suffering of others, or that we are in fact being targeted. By accepting that it is what it is, we can start understanding why it happened, what it did to us and how we can move on.

Radical acceptance is normally more effective in treating obviously severe and direct trauma such as assault. This is not to take away from the severity of more subtle trauma such as relational trauma—all trauma is valid, and every person handles trauma differently. Some find it easier to accept the trauma that happens with a bang, while others find the more subtle and more easily ignored trauma easier to accept. Radical acceptance can be used for all forms of trauma, and Dr. Marsha Linehan has come up with ten steps we can follow to achieve Radical Acceptance as part of a technique called Dialectical Behavior Therapy that she developed in the early 1970s:

- ☐ **Step 1: Observe –** You need to see your own situation and realize that something is not right, that you are having an argument against reality. This could present itself in multiple ways, such as cognitive dissonance. When you have thoughts along the lines of "It shouldn't be like this."

- ☐ **Step 2: The Reality –** Remind yourself of the unfortunate reality, and that it simply is what it is. This thing happened, and that's the uncomfortable truth.

- ☐ **Step 3: The Reason –** Remind yourself that something caused this—whether you know what or why does not matter, but there is a cause out there. This wasn't just a random occurrence that happened to affect you, it was an event that had causality.

☐ **Step 4: Practice – Practice** acceptance. You do not need to actually accept anything just yet. Just practice it while using techniques like acceptance, self-talk, relaxation techniques and imagery. This will help get you used to the idea of accepting what has happened.

☐ **Step 5: List –** Make a list of how you would change your behavior and what activities you would engage in if you were to accept the trauma. Then engage in these changes, start changing your behavior and do the activities as if you had already accepted your trauma.

☐ **Step 6: Imagine –** Close your eyes and imagine that you have already accepted your trauma. How would you feel, what would you do, where would you go and what would your life be like? Dream about this and let your mind wander.

☐ **Step 7: Attend –** Pay attention to the sensations in your body, the fear response, the pit in your stomach and especially the changes in your body while imagining that you have accepted this. Your body will tell you what to work on and where to focus when you pay attention to it.

☐ **Step 8: Allow –** Allow the emotions to be felt, the sadness, the grief, the disappointment and fear All these emotions that are awakened by the trauma, allow yourself to feel them.

☐ **Step 9: Acknowledge –** This trauma does not define you. Now is the time to acknowledge that you can live your life, even if you still have pain.

☐ **Step 10: Pros and Cons –** Make a list of the pros and cons if you were to accept the trauma, as well as a list of pros and cons if you were to not accept the trauma. Weigh up your options and see which will be the best.

With these steps you are well on your way to practice radical acceptance. Accepting the trauma is vital to being able to change the trauma. When we are able to admit that something bad happened to us, we are finally able to move past it. Saying that it's in the past allows us to move on. Moving on means moving towards healing.

CHAPTER 3:

TOXIC RELATIONSHIPS,

TRAUMA BONDING AND TIES

TO NARCISSISTS

Toxic relationships—everyone knows the term by now, and we often find that when media from as little as 20 years ago is viewed again, we see most of the relationships in them as being toxic. What few people understand, however, is that a toxic relationship does not have to be a sexual or romantic relationship, but can be a relationship between you and a co-worker or your boss; it can be the relationship with your instructor at the gym; a toxic relationship can develop between any two people in any situation as long as the correct personalities are involved.

NARCISSISTS AND EMPATHS

"When an accusation is thrown at you that does not fit you, when it doesn't capture what you know to be true about yourself or your behavior, mentally flip it back on your partner. He is likely accusing you of what he is doing or feeling. Accusations can be about the narcissist's own vulnerabilities and weaknesses."
— Ramani Durvasula

I would like to focus on two specific personalities. Most often toxic relationships exist around the typical empath and narcissist personality types, and these are the ones we will be looking at. We will start with the empath: These are the victims of these relationships.

Oftentimes, an empath will suffer from a toxic relationship from a young age; this is where their trauma bonding finds its roots. If at any time during their formative years the empath was part of a relationship where the other party would make conditional love clear (such as a grandparent refusing to show any type of affection unless the grandchild plays a certain sport or has a certain academic standing), the person will most probably enter into a toxic relationship later in life.

The narcissist, on the other hand, lacks key characteristics such as empathy; they will also only share their love under certain conditions, which will effectively have the empath begging for validation from the narcissist. This need for validation is how the narcissist exerts control over the empath. They will withhold their affection from this person more and more, each time changing the goalpost for when their victim is worthy of affection. These goalposts start out small, and seem completely normal; the narcissist will however gradually worsen them. I would like you to imagine, for example, starting a new hobby— say you decide to start sketching, and find out you are good at it. You move on from sketching in pencil to adding some color. Now that you can sketch, you decide to try and paint. You succeed, so you experiment with different paints, and then you see a technique on social media where somebody used oil-based paint to create a 3D painting, so you try that. Now look back: When you were just sketching with a pencil, you never thought you would be capable of creating 3D paintings. The narcissist will follow a similar route to make their victims feel that their behavior is normal, and it could be years before the victim realizes that this behavior is in fact not normal.

The empath will feel good every time they get a bit of approval from the narcissist, almost causing them to become addicted to this affection. As with any addiction, the empath will do whatever they can to get the affections from the narcissist. When the empath realizes that they are in a toxic relationship and are actually being abused, the narcissist will try to make them feel bad for attempting to get away from the environment.

RECOGNIZING A TOXIC RELATIONSHIP

"That said, if a person leads with charm and charisma and plenty of confidence, sit up straight and pay cautious attention. Make sure that there is empathy, that entitlement is not at play, that the person is genuine, that there is respect and, frankly, that he or she has the goods to back it up. Don't let the charisma and charm blind you and stop you from looking deeper for the rest of it." — Ramani Durvasula

We can normally recognize toxic relationships in the media, or outside our own homes quite easily. But oftentimes the closer to us the relationship is, the harder it is for us to recognize. One of the most common ways of recognizing that someone is in a toxic relationship is to look out for signs that they are being especially careful not to anger their partner. When someone is constantly walking on eggshells they are quite clearly fearing a negative reaction from their partner, sometimes without even realizing it.

Due to the fact that empaths and narcissists are not the only personality types that can be involved in toxic relationships, I will be referring to the controller and the victim to refer to those that are involved going forward.

Here are a few ways to recognize that someone may be walking on eggshells in a relationship:

- [ ] In social interactions, the victim will often be more quiet and defer questions and conversations to the controller.

- [ ] The victim will often, and in very subtle ways, ask the controller for permission before eating or drinking, especially when in a social environment.

- [ ] The victim will indulge themselves more in other addictive behavior, especially when the controller is not around.

- [ ] The victim will often withdraw completely from their friends and family, especially during times that they are not shown affection.

- [ ] The victim will not make any decisions without clearing them with the controller first, especially not when the controller is near. These will include small decisions such as what to eat and drink or even what ringtone they should have on their phone to not bother the controller.

You may realize that many of the signs someone is walking on eggshells are very similar to signs of depression. This is not a coincidence as one of the many results of a toxic relationship is that the victim will fall into a deep depression—but we'll look at this in more detail a bit later on.

There are some psychological theories that suggest that we all have a shadow and that a narcissist lives completely in that shadow, and that this is exactly what draws their victims to the narcissist. The idea is that the narcissist proudly displays those exact traits and aspects of your own personality that you completely and utterly reject and deny, that you are drawn to them as a way to find yourself.

Think of the narcissist as an actor. Place an actor anywhere and give them a script and they will most probably do a good job with it, but place them on a stage with props, and the art will be elevated to new levels. In this example we are the props: We are containers of all our unwanted qualities, and when paired with the actor, we create the perfect play.

Now I don't want you to feel bad or attacked by this—I am not calling you out, calling you a narcissist or telling you that you want to be a victim, I am actually complimenting you. If we accept that our Shadow Self is what makes the narcissist, that means that we have so rejected apathetic and toxic traits that we deny them from ourselves in an effort to be good people. This is the beauty of self-acceptance and Shadow Work. It allows us to accept these dark parts of ourselves and to use them in such a way that we do not become toxic or a negative influence on those around us. It also helps us to feel complete and fulfilled again so a narcissist cannot use the missing parts of ourselves to manipulate us into being their victims.

This may be one of the hardest writing prompts as this will probably be the prompt in which you will discover your Shadow Self the most, see the most negative parts of yourself and analyze them. I want you to be completely honest, but don't let it discourage you. Take your time, maybe take a bit of extra time doing this prompt, and try to make sure you plan an activity or something that you can do after this prompt to help you remain positive. Remember this is only part of the journey.

- [ ] What personality traits make up your Shadow Self?
- [ ] What is the worst trait you possess?
- [ ] Have you ever shown any narcissistic behavior?
- [ ] What traits of yourself have you seen reflected in a narcissist?
- [ ] How have you been dealing with these traits?
- [ ] How have you been working on improving these traits?
- [ ] How have you been ignoring these traits?
- [ ] What is it that draws you to a narcissist?
- [ ] How long does it take you to realize that you are dealing with a narcissist?

WRITING PROMPT: INTROSPECTION

Affirmation: Even the brightest of light shines a shadow, just as even the greatest of good has some bad in it.

Journal Prompt: My First Love

In this prompt I want you to think back to your first ever relationship and then explore it, looking at the things both of you did wrong, analyzing these and seeing whether they arose due to inexperience in dealing with relationships or due to behavioral issues on either side. Look at the partner you had: Did they show narcissistic traits? Did they cause you any trauma? Look at yourself: Did you cause them any trauma? How could you have acted differently during the relationship?

Victoria Stevens

MY FIRST LOVE

WHAT IS NARCISSISTIC PERSONALITY DISORDER?

"Betrayal. A breach of trust. Fear. What you thought was true—counted on to be true—was not. It was just smoke and mirrors, outright deceit and lies. Sometimes it was hard to tell because there was just enough truth to make everything seem right. Even a little truth with just the right spin can cover the outrageous. Worse, there are the sincerity and care that obscure what you have lost. You can see the outlines of it now. It was exploitation. You were used. Everything in you wants to believe you weren't." — Patrick J. Carnes

No healing can happen if we do not understand the cause of our pain first. To understand this, how it happens and why, we need to look at exactly what NPD (Narcissistic Personality Disorder) is. In short, a narcissist is someone that is not only self-important and who feeds on the constant adoration and attempts of approval from their victim, but also has a broken moral compass and complete apathy towards them. They cannot accept general critique and often become extremely agitated when they do not receive the special attention they feel entitled to. Unlike some other personality disorders, with NPD, the person is themselves always in control, retains the recollection of everything they do and can feel emotion. But, just like other disorders, they don't necessarily see anything wrong with their actions.

The cause of NPD is still unclear and greatly debated. It has been connected to genetics, indicating that a genetic marker or disorder could lead to NPD. It has also been connected to neurobiology, suggesting that there could be an issue in the way that those with NPD think: Somewhere between the brain, thinking and their actual behavior there is a disconnect that leads to the actions of a narcissist. Finally the last connection is environment. Often this is blamed on parents either giving too much attention to and spoiling their kids, or excessive criticism very similar to that of their victims where a definite lack of affection is clear. It is sometimes believed that a narcissist starts to imitate the environment that they grew up in, but, unlike empaths continuously imitating the victim side of the environment, they instead imitate the abusive side of the environment.

I mention empaths here because, as I have said, there are several similarities between narcissists and empaths, from relational trauma and ACE's playing key roles in their early years to their attraction toward each other and their tendencies to becoming addicted to toxic relationships.

The main difference between a narcissist and an empath, however, is that they tend to become polar opposites to each other. Where an empath fully and completely embraces the emotions of the other person, while they bottle up and internalize their insecurities and then work to identify the struggles of those around them in order to help even at great cost to themselves, a narcissist utterly rejects the emotions of others, turning their focus inward to ensure that their emotions are the ones that are looked after. They project their insecurities and fears on those around them and then break those people down for presenting these feelings. They ensure that they are kept content and disregard the cost to those around them.

I do not want you to feel sorry or forgive narcissists, although it is true that they usually have their own demons to fight off. When you forgive them, though, and show them that you are sorry, as an empath you will find yourself back at their mercy. They will not see the good you are doing or allow you to help them, but will instead use this against you again. I have found that it is quite important we understand narcissists and why they are the way they are—as well as why empaths are their victims of choice—so that we can accept this situation and the pain that we were in, and eventually move on from it.

it's
OK
not to be
OK

Self and our similarities with narcissists. Now I want you to reaffirm your faith in yourself, recognize that you are in fact not a narcissist, and pay attention to the differences. I want you to find a balance between the good and the bad in yourself and see where you can accept both and let your full and true self emerge.

☐ What are traits you possess that a narcissist will never possess?

☐ What are the key differences between you and a narcissist?

☐ What makes you a good person?

☐ What have you recently done that a narcissist would never do? (Here I would like to point out that if you have not had the emotional energy to do anything, that is okay. Empaths run on emotional energy, and victims of narcissistic abuse are normally drained emotionally. Anxiety and depression can make doing anything a hard and scary task, but even thinking of someone else and their well-being, showing an ounce of concern, is already more than what a narcissist will do, and that does count!)

☐ Why do you think you differ so much from a narcissist?

☐ What is the moment in your life where you were the proudest of yourself?

☐ What is the most selfless thing you have ever done in your life?

Writing Prompt: Reaffirmation

WRITING PROMPT: REAFFIRMATION

Affirmation: As long as I am actively trying to be a good person, I'm already succeeding.

Journal Prompt: A Letter to my Abusers

This may be a very difficult one to write, but I want you to let your thoughts out towards all those people that have caused you trauma, pain, and devastation. I want you to let them have it, let them know exactly who and what you think they are, the good, the bad, the happy and the sad. Don't worry about achieving a specific goal, just let your feelings go.

A LETTER TO MY ABUSERS

ARE YOU IN LOVE OR IS IT JUST TRAUMA-BONDING?

To understand these relationships we'll have to investigate actual love and trauma bonding and how both of these present themselves. The first way to do that is to look at the seven stages of trauma bonding.

Stage 1: Love Bombing

This is the absolute start of the relationship. From the moment you meet the narcissist, the love bombing stage starts. During this stage you are absolutely and completely showered in love, so much that you feel completely overwhelmed and taken aback that someone this perfect can exist. In romantic relationships, they present themselves as your perfect counterpart. In more professional relationships, they present themselves as your perfect colleague, the work bestie that is always there for you, who will cover for you and help out whenever you need anything.

Stage 2: The Hook

In the first stage, the narcissist will make the relationship all about you. During stage two, the focus will start shifting to them. They will start pushing you into situations where you rely on them. In a relationship, they will try to get you to move in with them and assure you that it is definitely not happening too fast, that this is the best option for you. They will use excuses like "Think of how much money you will save". In a more professional setting, this may be presented as a carpool opportunity: "If we drive together, just think of how much fuel you can save". This can also include other situations that may break down the professional walls, such as invites to their family barbecue or an invite for drinks after work.

Then when you start spending time with them, and they feel you are starting to need them and want to be around them, they will start distancing themselves. In a romantic relationship, this could be just suddenly becoming quiet and emotionally distant but will be explained away as them needing to adjust to living with someone. Or suddenly they have to work late or on their off days, and plans for the evening or the entire day are suddenly canceled. In a more professional relationship, they suddenly can't help you with something at work, or will let you know at the last moment that they cannot pick you up for work or drop you off afterwards.

This is where the divide between a normal loving relationship and trauma bonding starts to come in. The narcissist will be testing the water and ensuring that they have effectively got you addicted to them, and in small amounts distance themselves bit by bit so that you keep craving their love and validation and not directly realize that they are trying to make you suffer from withdrawal symptoms.

Stage 3: Breaking You Down

In stage one you have been built up; in stage two the narcissist has established the fact that you need them. In this stage, they deepen that addiction you have towards them. You have a need for their affection, so what happens when you receive the exact opposite? Contrary to popular belief, you actually find yourself with a need to change their disdain into praise again.

Think of it as going to a restaurant everyday and always ordering your favorite meal, and receiving the best tasting dish ever to be created. Then suddenly for a few days they don't have a key ingredient, and when they do get the ingredient again, the dish suddenly does not taste as good. You know how good it can taste, and you know no other restaurant can even get close. So you start craving the quality you had gotten used to. What would you do to get that quality back? Would you pay more for it? Would you come in earlier or later than your usual time if you are guaranteed that quality? What if they told you the chef loves the color orange and always puts in extra effort for a customer wearing an orange shirt? It's not that hard to just wear an orange shirt or jersey to get what you want.

This is what happens in the third stage. Without you realizing it, the narcissist starts breaking you down, criticizing you and devaluing you. At first you may just think that they are giving you constructive criticism because your relationship has finally become comfortable enough that you can be honest with each other.

They'll start out small, telling you that you would look better once you get a haircut, or that you don't drive that badly but they are definitely the better driver. This will gradually increase, they will become more and more demanding, they will set higher and higher goals for you before they are pleased again, and finally anytime they are unhappy or something goes wrong, it will be your fault.

In a romantic relationship, this could start out as something like telling you that you are doing the dishes wrong; it will eventually move to telling you that you are disgustingly dirty, you smell up the place and leave the place dirty just by walking through it. You will be blamed for all the dishes in the sink, you will be blamed for all the dust and you will be blamed for them feeling negative about coming home at night, because they know there is a dirty house waiting for them and that affects their mental health.

In a more professional relationship, it could start off with them giving you simple ways to improve your quality of work. It will then escalate into you not being able to do your work at all; you are completely incompetent and can't do anything right. If anything at work goes wrong, a customer, manager or employer is unhappy, then you will be blamed. If the narcissist makes a mistake at work or gets into trouble over their work, it will be your fault because they had to fix your mistakes, or your poor quality of work made everyone else unhappy and caused the overall work to be poor. No matter what you do the blame will be worked back to you.

Stage 4: Gaslighting

It is only natural to start feeling like something may be wrong during the third stage. Your feelings start to get hurt, you start to feel like you are not good enough, you start to wonder if this relationship is right for you. Since we are all trying to be decent people and handle any situation in a mature way, the natural reaction here is to open a conversation with the other party and explain our fears and thoughts. This is when the narcissist needs to take the final step to change your thoughts and emotions so that you completely belong to them. They achieve this through gaslighting you.

I understand that 'gaslighting' is a relatively new term, and although most people have become so accustomed to the term, it is not always recognised. Gaslighting is when the abuser uses your words and thoughts and twists them until they have turned it back on you, then uses that to cause you to doubt yourself. I'll use an example from the previous stage to better explain how this is achieved: In the romantic scenario I used the example of doing the dishes and the abuser telling you that you don't do it correctly, and eventually that being used to insult your hygiene and telling you that you are causing the abuser to not want to be at home at all because of its poor state. Eventually, with your feelings hurt, you will approach them and tell them that their words are hurtful and make you feel like you are dirty and incapable of doing basic tasks. Instead of hearing you out, they will turn your words around, telling you that you are making them out to be a liar; they will accuse you of making them sound ridiculous and then blame you for not taking their feelings into account. You may try to argue that you are taking their feelings into account, but don't feel like yours are being taken into account, but your words will still be turned against you again. By the end of the argument you will feel like you are the abuser and that your feelings are ridiculous. This will lead to what is called "cognitive dissonance".

Cognitive dissonance is a mental conflict that causes great confusion in a person especially when they believe two separate but completely contradictory things, such as that they are abusing the person that is abusing them.

This is a very important stage in trauma-bonding as this is the last stage used to gain control over you. After this, the rest of the trauma-bonding is ways of keeping control. This brings us to the next phase.

Stage 5: Resignation & Submission

This is the stage where you realize that no matter how you approach it, having a logical and open discussion with your abuser is completely impossible. No matter how hard you try or what you do, you just cannot reason with a narcissist.

After this entire time of trying, fighting, thinking up new ways to try and peacefully sort out the issues, you are so completely and utterly exhausted both mentally and emotionally that you just give up. You stop the fighting and hope that, by submitting to their will, you'll get them to go back to stage one. If you just keep quiet and wash that dish an extra time, if you stay up a bit later and work on that report for a couple more hours, if you just fix the part of yourself that they are unhappy with, you will make them happy again, and then they will be that nice person again, making it all worthwhile.

By doing this, you give the abuser the power to disrespect you and to break you down. Resigning to them confirms their power over you. This is the sign to them that they can continue their abuse with no restrictions and, no matter how hard you try, achieving their affection will from now on be next to impossible and the goal post will be higher than ever.

Stage 6: Loss of Self

You have now gotten to the point where you have started to accept that nothing you do will ever result in a productive conversation or help to sort out the issues in your relationship. This means you have stopped trying, and now all your thoughts and energy are focused on pleasing this person, doing whatever you can to make them happy—but due to the fact that this will never actually happen you are *constantly* trying to make them happy. Your friends and family will probably have started realizing that something is wrong during stage three.

This is when they start seeing issues, but since they are not being targeted by the abuser, they will still be too uncomfortable to say anything and too unsure of the situation to directly address it. By this stage, they may be both sure and willing enough to intervene and say something, but you will be so exhausted from feeling powerless that you ignore their fears, warnings and interjections. You are already so hooked on the abuser and used to their abuse that it all seems normal and will probably reassure those close to you that nothing is wrong.

Unfortunately, many will still feel that something is not right and that pushing the conversation will either cause friction between you and them. At the same time, you will feel that they are causing problems in your relationship, pressuring you into something you do not want, or that they do not want to see you happy and are trying to sabotage your life.

This will lead you to spending less time with them and withdrawing from your social life and circumstances. Having this free time, it's only natural to expect that you will be using this to focus on yourself and your hobbies. The problem with this, though, is that by now you are so scared of inconveniencing the abuser and so focused on perfecting whatever task and environment they expect from you that instead of focusing on yourself, you shift your focus to the abuser.

You finally start to completely neglect yourself and only focus on them. Your self-esteem will be so low that you see yourself as less important than them in any situation. This is how you start losing yourself. Before you realize it, your entire existence is focused on your abuser, and your interests and hobbies are discarded in favor of ensuring their happiness and comfort.

By this stage, you become a shadow of your former self, hiding in the shadow of the abuser.

Stage 7: Emotional Addiction

Like with any addiction, you need to keep hooked so that you do not realize that you can live without your addiction. This is the final stage. You will be kept on such a roller coaster that you sometimes go months stuck in an anxiety ridden stage of stress where you find absolutely no joy in anything. Then that one time that they give you love and affection you feel so euphoric and elated again that this can keep you going for months again. You suddenly feel relieved from the pain and depression that had you hiding from the world, you have this new rejuvenated feeling and so much energy that you channel towards your abuser to thank them for making you feel like this. It takes you a while to realize that you have been on a downer and have been losing your happiness, but just before you care enough to make the connection, they feed your addiction again.

This is a cycle narcissists go through and the entire goal of this cycle is to keep their victim under their control and at their mercy. The cycle will often interchange between stage one and stage three, going from love bombing the victim to breaking them down and back again.

This is the final stage of trauma-bonding, and this is the stage that closes the trap on the victim. Once the victim has gotten to this stage of the trauma-bond, they find it so difficult to escape that it is nearly impossible. By this stage, the victim is so brainwashed and manipulated that they believe themselves to be completely in love with their abuser and completely dependent on them.

"A narcissist hates you wholeheartedly
and thoroughly simply because you are."
— Sam Vaknin

Victoria Stevens
WHAT IS LOVE?

"When we are free, we can look in the face of our cravings and desires and say 'I don't have to satisfy you'." — Marsha M. Linehan

The main misconception that is drilled into the mind of the victim is that the trauma-bond they feel with their abuser is actual love. It's quite easy to make someone believe what we want them to when it comes to love. The reason for this is that love cannot actually be defined any more than through a general meaning. The Merriam-Webster dictionary has several definitions for the word 'love', my favorite being, "affection based on admiration and benevolence". The problem with this definition is that it describes exactly the feelings that the victim has towards the abuser, but not the feeling that the abuser reciprocates.

Aside from the literal definition, love is also an emotion and the way it presents itself and makes a person feel differs for each and every individual. Love is an imperfect situation; it will never be tit for tat or look the same from day to day. The one fact about love is, however, that it should always result in happiness.

One thing that I am sure of is that even during the good and the bad, the fights and the happy times, both parties should feel comfortable and happy. I won't say that there should never be a moment when either party questions the relationship, because it is only human to question ourselves from time to time. That being said, love should help you to get out of bed every morning, not be the reason you want to stay in it all day.

As long as both parties feel positive and work together to encourage and build up each other wherever possible, it is love. The key point here is that both parties are equally as important, not just one.

In this writing prompt I want you to try and find yourself again; I want you to channel your inner child as well as your superficial qualities. Be completely honest with yourself and find every aspect about yourself. Look at the good and look at the bad, look at everything in between. Identify what makes you, you. In essence these will be the identifiers of your personality.

- ❏ What is your biggest quality, what is the one thing everyone remembers or always knows about you?

- ❏ What is the one part of yourself you want to make sure you will never change for anyone?

- ❏ What six aspects of your personality are most important to create your self identity? The good and the bad?

- ❏ How much have you changed from when you were a child?

- ❏ Knowing signs of a toxic relationship, were you in a similar situation as a child? Where, when, how and with who?

- ❏ Thinking back, what did love mean to you as a child?

- ❏ Does love still mean the same thing to you?

- ❏ Who are the people you would trust completely to tell you that they think a relationship is detrimental to your health?

- ❏ Think back to being an adult: Do you ever feel that you were in a toxic relationship?

- ❏ Is there currently any relationship in your life that shows signs of trauma-bonding?

- ❏ Write out 5 hard limit points that will work as a checklist to make sure you never get involved in trauma-bonding again.

WRITING PROMPT: YOU

WRITING PROMPT: YOU

Affirmation: I am me, and nobody can be a better me than I am.

Journal Prompt: Relationships

Look at yourself, at the type of person you are, the type of person you dream of and reflect on that. I want this prompt to be a fantasy piece for you. Dream a bit, let that kid take over again that used to dream about what a relationship and your adult life would be like for you, and then write down your fantasy. I want you to envision the perfect relationship, the positive relationship. Just don't be scared to write any emotions and fantasies you have—but when you realize that you are fantasizing about aspects that could be negative, ensure that they are still written down and then crossed out so that when you look back at this at a later stage you can recognize the negatives and see how you have changed and grown.

A good idea may be to write out that one moment you think would make an impression on you and make you realize a relationship is perfect. Think of a day where things may go extremely wrong for you and where you may be at your lowest. What would you like your perfect partner to do, how do you want them to make you feel better and, if you were to be honest with yourself, what is the one thing they would be able to do to immediately change your mood?

As an example, I would think of being dismissed from work, at the same time receiving the millionth rejection letter from a publisher about my next book and hearing that a close family member has passed away. For me that would have me at my absolute lowest, but my perfect partner would take me in their arms, let me cry a bit and afterwards offer to give me a big bowl of ice cream. Then, right before they give me my ice cream, they would deliberately drop it in my lap. I would be mad at first, I would start yelling about how that is absolutely mean of them and completely inappropriate. I was looking forward to that ice cream, and I do not even have the money to go out and buy more. The entire time while I am screaming and yelling, and eventually crying about it, my partner would stand in front of me with a childlike smile, and when I am ugly crying and no longer making sense, and all the ice cream on me has started melting, they would scoop it up with their hands and smear it all over me and start laughing uncontrollably. Then I would start laughing, then crying, then laughing and eventually do both at the same time while my partner looks at me and tells me that they have faith in me and that I will be able to get back on top of the world pretty soon. I would not want them to tell me that they will take care of it, I would not want them to tell me that they will make everything fine, I would not want them to tell me that they will look after me. Instead I would want them to support me, get to know my personality and how to help me be their equal instead of having them look after me.

I realize this may be a bit of a tall order, but I want you to dream, let out your Shadow Self, that part that you hide from the world, that part you tend to ignore. Let that part of you take over for this bit.

RELATIONSHIPS

CHAPTER 4:

SETTING THOSE BOUNDARIES

"Deep down, below the surface of the average man's conscience, he hears a voice whispering, 'There is something not right,' no matter how much his rightness is supported by public opinion or moral code." — Carl Gustav Jung

Now that we know what to look out for, and how we can end up in these horrible situations, we need to start looking at how to never get in these circumstances again. The only way to do this is to set up boundaries. These won't be the boundaries like those in a movie or series, but actual boundaries that can be followed and respected as well as understood by any person that values you and your emotions.

These boundaries should not only be set for the future, but also be applied to those already in your life. As we have already established, those most prone to trauma-bonding and toxic relationships are those that have suffered from them in their formative years. This can include siblings, parents, grandparents, old friends and even co-workers.

More importantly, many of the limits and boundaries you need to implement could be upon yourself. This is not only to protect you from toxic relationships, but to protect yourself and others from your own personal toxic or negative traits.

FIND YOUR LIMITS AND NEEDS

"The best way to choose the wrong door, or never even open the door, is to let fear run the show. When you reflect on any big-ticket decision you have made on the basis of fear and anxiety, you can almost guarantee you made the wrong decision." — Ramani Durvasula

The main questions you are probably asking yourself right now are how do I find my limits, how do I implement them, and how do they fit in with my needs? To establish the answers, we need to look at what our actual needs are. I would like to bring another term in here, but this term requires thorough looking at and explanation.

"High maintenance" is a term that is often seen as a toxic trait, and although it can be, it can also be a coping mechanism for those that have suffered from poor relationships in their past. Being high maintenance, however, does have a fine line between being healthy and okay, and being toxic and detrimental.

You will have to take a long hard look at yourself and determine whether or not you are a high maintenance person, and how healthy you are in this manner. Being high maintenance can mean that you feel you need more constant attention than others would see as normal; you may be a bit more clingy. This can be perfectly fine if not taken too far. I could write several books on this topic alone and still not get to the point, but as you may realize I have found that one of the best ways to make a point is through examples. So I'll go into an example again.

Let's say in this scenario you are involved in a relationship with a romantic partner. This partner does not check the boxes to qualify for NPD and has never initiated a trauma-bond with you. Despite all this, you still feel a constant need to receive attention from your partner; when you do not feel this attention you start to become anxious, you start to doubt yourself, you start to worry about your own value. This is you being high maintenance. In a healthy scenario, an ideal outcome would be constant communication with your partner, admitting your flaws and listening when your partner tells you that you may be overreacting a bit. A toxic outcome would be that, whenever this happens, you look for a flaw in your partner and argue with them with the intent that within a few minutes you would make up with them, and this would mean that they have to give you affection to prove to you that everything is okay again, or you restrict them from doing something because it causes you more anxiety.

In the example I have given I would like to point out that there is still a form of emotion on your side, and that you are not void of emotions and simply attempting to control your partner. Instead, even during the toxic scenario you are attempting to give your partner affection instead of keeping it from them. That is where the major difference between a person with NPD and a toxic high maintenance person comes in.

Now that you know where you are on the scale of being high maintenance, what are your needs in this regard? As an example, I would say that someone who is high maintenance could set a healthy need of at least one kiss, one hug and one "I love you" from their partner per day. This could help to serve as a tool to reassure you every day that you are in a loving relationship and can help you to lessen the anxiety you start to feel when you think you are not getting enough attention. In this way, it also sets a limit for you; our partners also have their own emotions and feelings, and may not always be able to give us a high quantity of the affection that we may feel we need. In order to take their needs and boundaries into consideration, if we limit ourselves we also show them that their feelings and needs are important and they do not feel like we are suffocating them or forcing them into a situation that will drain them.

I used high maintenance as a very specific example because, as I said, it is a trait that can be toxic—but it is also a trait that can be a result of the environment and trauma that causes us to become involved in these types of relationships later on, and, especially for a high maintenance person, the love bombing and gaslighting stages are especially effective on them.

Being high maintenance is not the only trait that we might possess that can be seen as a result of our trauma, a tool to be used against us, or a toxic trait.

We need to look deeper into ourselves and see what other traits we possess, why we have them and how we can limit ourselves to help create a healthy environment around us.

Once we start radiating a healthy environment, we need to look at the atmosphere around us. Is this healthy enough for us to thrive in? What can we change to make it a healthier environment? This is where our boundaries come in. These boundaries can be light boundaries, such as ensuring that we make time for ourselves and our hobbies, to going full no-contact with certain people.

Soft Boundaries

Let's start by taking a look at soft boundaries. A soft boundary can be something like setting aside one hour per week for a specific activity. This can be any activity that gives you a sense of self. Don't think of this as a time in which you have to be productive or do anything at all. You can use this time to just soak in a bath and think of the week, or go to a movie; you could even use this time to yell into the void until you lose your voice. The idea is to set a soft boundary to keep in touch with yourself. You won't be imposing on anyone, you won't be making anyone uncomfortable and you won't be taking time away from anyone else. An hour a week is all you need; you don't need to schedule the hour at the same time on the same day of every week, and you can keep it fluid and do it whenever best suits you.

Moderate Boundaries

A moderate boundary will look a bit more obvious. It may impose slightly on someone but should still be done in a respectful manner. An example of this would be if you are working longer hours than your partner, it would not be too much to ask them to take up more duties around the house than you, without complaint.

If there are children involved, acknowledgment of reproductive labor should be always kept in strong consideration. If any job gets criticized all the time, then the other partner should take it on going forward. With families and friends, if the partner is not in a good mood or always makes negative remarks, s/he either does not attend events or changes their attitude. These are just some examples of how to create some moderate boundaries that will inevitably create some more healthy space for you (and your children if applicable) to live in.

Hard Boundaries

Now we need to look at hard boundaries. They are not just called hard boundaries because you should be infallible in them, but also because these are the hardest boundaries to keep in place. These are the boundaries that require you to take a long and hard look at your life. You are radiating a healthy environment, you made the atmosphere around you healthy and now you need to pull out the weeds that feed off you. These are the ones that are clearly toxic to you, and I feel it important to point out to you that this can be anyone: a new partner, an old friend, a new work acquaintance and anyone in between.

If the toxic person is a partner and s/he continues to be abusive, writing emails to them is also a good idea to document your struggles (and they can be used in court should you need to divorce). Remember that nobody knows what happens behind closed doors, but it is your right to feel safe, loved, and ultimately happy.

We have looked at all the signs and stages of a toxic relationship, and if you have anyone in your life that ticks these boxes, you should take severe action. Yes, no-contact is a part of hard boundaries, but we will look at that separately in a moment. There are other options to explore as well.

Let's use the workplace as an example. A colleague is ticking these boxes and proving to be a negative influence in your life. What do you do? This co-worker may be trying to force themselves on you, interject in your life and control your work. You will need the courage to face them head on and keep your relationship professional. To do this I would personally suggest sending them a text or email saying that you want to take a step back and clearly keep the relationship as it should be. From there on, keep all communications in a format in which you can prove they occurred. A narcissist will not take kindly to being told to step back and will instead try to find a way to keep you under their control, whether this is by telling you that your work is subpar or telling the company that you are the one being abusive toward them. When that does not work, they will sweet talk and manipulate you into reinstating the previous status-quo. They will start the love bombing stage again and work on you to try and get you back, but once

Victoria Stevens

you are they will very quickly go back to their old ways.

You will need to keep your boundaries in place as long as this person is in your life in some way. These boundaries will need to be completely clear and you will need some sort of coping mechanism to help you with them. This coping mechanism can be anything from a friend, partner or family member who is there for you, or it could be a way that you help yourself. Perhaps look into something like writing yourself a letter or making a video to yourself in which you are completely honest with yourself, break down and let every little feeling out and then record it so that whenever you feel that you may waiver in your convictions of these boundaries, you remember why you put them in place.

I want you to explore your needs and boundaries. Look at what you need, where you overstep and where others transgress. Where do your needs cripple you and where do they break boundaries from others? How will you change your life? How will all these changes affect your life both positively and negatively?

- ☐ Make a list of every emotional need you have no matter how big or small.

- ☐ What are traits you possess that can be seen as toxic?

- ☐ How can you improve these needs to make them less toxic?

- ☐ Set three boundaries for your life: one soft, one moderate and one hard.

- ☐ Think hard: Has anyone ever set any boundaries that you have crossed by accident?

- ☐ Now be honest, none of us are perfect: Have you ever on purpose disregarded someone's boundaries?

- ☐ Who would be the people most impacted by your new boundaries?

- ☐ What will you do with your new boundaries and the time they will give you to yourself?

- ☐ What will be your hardest boundary to set and why?

WRITING PROMPT: EXPLORATION

WRITING PROMPT: EXPLORATION

Journal Prompt: Meanings

Look at boundaries, look at what they signify and what they could mean. Now go away from the facts and definitions and look into yourself. What do boundaries mean to you? Be honest with yourself and reflect on how your life will change. Be stern and be real, but dream about how much your life will improve with your boundaries in place. In the writing prompt we looked at what boundaries you would place in your life and why. Now we will look at their results and what the endgame is here. Let your dreams out and let your mind wander.

MEANINGS

Find Your Limits and Needs

GOING NO-CONTACT, AND STICKING TO IT

"Perhaps the hardest thing of all is to leave the illusion. A part of what you are leaving is an illusion, a mirage—something that actually is not there. And it is not real. And yet, it hurts. Ending a relationship is stressful, challenging, and psycho-logically difficult. Whether it has been going on for months or years, breaking up is hard to do. We consider issues, including what we are getting out of our relationship, whether there is someone else out there who might be better for us who is available and a good option, as well as what we might lose if we left. We do that algebra of the heart and if the numbers favor staying, we stay. If the numbers favor leaving, we leave." — Ramani Durvasula

In the section on hard boundaries, we touched on no-contact. It is now time to expand on this approach for setting boundaries, and we'll start off with what it means. No-contact is pretty self explanatory: We completely cut someone out of our lives and break off any and all contact with this person. We stop seeing them, we stop responding to their messages, we stop giving them any energy whatso-ever.

Why would we do this? This is an extreme reaction that should be reserved for the most extreme of circumstances. You would only do this when the person is com-pletely toxic to you, when they completely disregard you and your emotions. If you cut out too many people, and for no reason, you could end up cutting your-self off from the world and cause more damage than good. That said, do not let anyone tell you that you should not be cutting another person from your life. This is a personal choice that only you can make based on the relationship that you (and *only you*) have with someone.

Quite often the people that someone in this situation would go no-contact with are family or friends that have been 'close' to them for a long time. When this happens—especially in regards to family you are often faced with—comments along the line of "It's your mom, you should always love her," or "You two have been friends forever, you can't just throw away friendship like that" may come up often. Comments like these are meant to be helpful and come from a good place, but they usually result in the victim of a toxic relationship suffering further instead of allowing them to heal.

What many people fail to realize is that a parent can cause damage, a grand-parent can be toxic and continuing these relationships can have a long-term negative effect on a person. This negative effect will be even more severe if the toxicity of the relationship and its subsequent abuse is still ongoing.

To understand this more I'll give you the example of an emotionally distant mother that never believes her child is good enough or qualified enough for anything in life. If they tell her that they are trying out for their school debate team, the mother will be unsupportive and tell them that they will not win any debate. If they tell her that they are looking to rent an apartment, the mother will tell them they should look for something cheap that they'll be able to afford when they eventually lose their job. When they tell her they are dating someone, she will ask them what is wrong with the person and why they would want to date someone like her kid? This mother is not nurturing and helping her children, but instead breaking them down, causing them trauma and grooming them for future abusive relationships. A parent like this will often not end their terror and will continue to break their kids down even as adults.

These are the relationships that you should be looking out for, and ask yourself whether or not these relationships should be cut off completely and should go no-contact, or if hard boundaries will work.

When you do go no-contact with someone, the important thing to do is to stick with the decision. That person will do whatever they can to try and get back in your life. A parent will use other family members to guilt trip you, and if that does not work, they will be patient, they will wait for their chance, and then use major events such as family celebrations or family tragedies to regain control over you. It often takes them only one conversation to convince you to let them back into your life, and it's just as fast for the abuse to start again. This is why keeping to no-contact is important once you start with it.

YOU DIDNT COME THIS FAR TO ONLY COME THIS FAR

The first 100 days are the most crucial; during this time the abuser still focuses on you, and believes that they have a chance to get back control. It is also during this time that you will suffer from withdrawal from them and actually miss them. In this prompt I want you to look at all aspects of what might happen during this time period.

- ☐ How would you break off contact? Would you tell them or just stop contact?

- ☐ How would you stop them from reaching out to you by just showing up to your house?

- ☐ Think forward: How long will it take them to accept the new relationship? Will they ever accept it?

- ☐ In the first 30 days, how often would you have to change your life and plans to avoid this person?

- ☐ Between 30 and 60 days, how would you react to someone telling you that you now have had enough time to calm down and should be able to forgive them?

- ☐ After 60 days, how many of those that are or were close to both of you would still accept and respect your choice?

- ☐ How would you deal with the questions during this time of why you decided to end this relationship?

- ☐ Be truthful to yourself: Do you think that you would be able to last 100 days without this person? Why or why not?

WRITING PROMPT:

THE FIRST HUNDRED DAYS

WRITING PROMPT:

THE FIRST HUNDRED DAYS

Journal Prompt: The Action Plan

Now that you have determined who you need to break contact with and how to deal with it, write it down. Create a plan of action ranging from breaking contact to keeping no-contact. While you are doing this, also look at your reasoning behind it again; when thoughts of what this person did to you and how it made you feel pop up, write that down and then make a plan of what you think you can do to get rid of those feelings, how you can heal yourself, and then explain to yourself why it is important to rectify this.

THE ACTION PLAN

SELF-CARE, TRUST AND RECONNECTING WITH YOUR BODY

"What if I should discover that the poorest of the beggars and the most impudent of offenders are all within me; and that I stand in need of the alms of my own kindness, that I, myself, am the enemy who must be loved—what then?" —
Carl Gustav Jung

By reading this book and doing research on how to heal, how to break the cycle and how to get away from toxic people and situations, you have already started on your self-care journey. Unfortunately, self-care is a journey that will never come to an end. You will continuously be working—healing yourself from new wounds as well as old—and there will always be new tools and new techniques to use. We focused on using Shadow Work in this book. I know that Shadow Work is effective and that it can have a positive influence on you, but this is only one of many tools available to you. You should use whatever feels right to you to continuously care for your inner self.

By using this book as a guide, you are already taking the first steps. By doing things like setting boundaries, taking some time for yourself and breaking away from abuse, you are not only practicing self-care, but also succeeding at it!

By now you should realize that those who have been in toxic relationships and had trauma-bonding experiences, even if it was just once, suffer from trust issues. You often find yourself wondering if you are receiving actual affection or only being love bombed again. You will need to take steps to regain trust in those around you, as well as yourself. Once you have gained a healthy circle of people around you and created a nourishing environment for yourself, you will have created a constructive environment in which you will be able to regain trust. It may take time and it may be a long and difficult road, but trust is vital to having any sort of healthy environment.

You will also need to reconnect with your body. There is a reason you are often told to trust your gut; this is because your body directly shows signs of your emotions and feelings. When you are happy you feel a lightness in your chest, you feel energized and your heart rate increases. When you are unhappy, you feel tired and exhausted, your body feels heavy and your heart rate drops. Every emotion has an impact and causes changes in your body. While you were undergoing abuse and reconditioning through manipulation by narcissists using techniques such as trauma-bonding, you were forced to ignore your body, to change how it reacts to your emotions and to eventually switch it off so that your emotions and reactions better aligned with the wishes of the one controlling you. Now, you need to not only let out your inner self, but you must also let it speak and learn to listen to it again.

You need to recondition yourself once more so that your body starts to react normally, and you can learn to understand these feelings and what they mean. Think of it as similar to someone that was severely injured undergoing physical therapy: They must learn how to walk again, they must learn what pain feels like and how to move their body. You may still have full control over your body, but the signals it sends to your brain no longer make sense. This is yet another reason why doing things like taking a long bath alone, or discussing your week and how it made you feel with your partner are important. The more you reflect on these emotions and feelings, the more you focus on them and the more you push yourself to feel them again, the more you will trust your body to react correctly and naturally and the more you will reconnect with your inner self.

In this writing prompt I want you to draw parallels and compare the feelings you had and the reactions your body had before you were in the toxic relationship and how it felt after you were reconditioned. Each and every emotion is important, and each and every reaction of your body as well.

- ☐ Make a list of every emotion you can think of, and under each emotion write down how it used to make you feel and how it makes you feel now.

- ☐ Assess every emotion and feeling, and determine when you felt it correctly

- ☐ See if there are any emotions you have never felt any differently.

- ☐ Explore why these emotions may not be different: Was it caused by childhood reconditioning?

- ☐ How do you know what emotions should feel like? (If you are unsure here, search it and see if your guess is correct.)

WRITING PROMPT: THE BODY

WRITING PROMPT: THE BODY

Journal Prompt: Love Yourself

I want you to flirt with yourself. I want you to build yourself up and make yourself feel all giddy and happy. Compliment your body, your personality and your life. Look at your achievements and write down all the good and amazing stuff you have done in your life. In this prompt I want you to really and truly love yourself in each and every aspect. Pay special attention to the things that have been used against you, and the things that were used to break you down. How can you improve your perception of these traits and how can you turn them into something positive? Once you figure it out, write it down and turn that pain and hatred into love and purity.

LOVE YOURSELF

49

CHAPTER 5: AWAKEN YOUR AUTHENTICITY

WHAT IS AN EMPATH?

"The meaning of my existence is that life has addressed a question to me. Or, conversely, I myself am a question which is addressed to the world, and I must communicate my answer, for otherwise I am dependent upon the world's answer." — Carl Gustav Jung

We've already touched on what an empath is. but I would like to give this a lot more attention. Empaths are people that (as the name explains) feel a greater amount of empathy towards another, more so than the average person usually does. When someone walks into a room, an empath can usually immediately pick up on their current feelings and emotions. They may not always realize that they are picking up on these emotions as they become so used to it that they do so subconsciously.

How empathy works is a great debate. Some believe that this is a supernatural occurrence where the empath can feel the energy that another living being exerts and recognize it; others believe that these are highly observant individuals that notice the body language, expressions and minor changes in the body of those around them. Whichever the reason, the reality is that the empath will recognize the feelings of another more easily, and these feelings will have an impact on the emotions and feelings of the empath.

This is one of the reasons why empaths normally have careers that allow them to directly interact with people; jobs like bartending allow the empath to use this ability to their advantage. By being able to properly gauge the emotions of their clientele, they are able to better communicate with their patrons and see trouble coming before anyone else. This allows them to completely excel at their careers.

The problem with this is, however, that it is also a lot easier for a narcissist to influence the emotions of the empath, making them easier to control and manipulate emotionally. Due to the fact that empaths feel emotions more intensely than normal people, it also speeds up the process and makes them the main targets for narcissists.

In this prompt I want you to explore your own empathy, whether you are an empath or not. For this exercise you will have to look around you and at those around you. Try and pick radically different personality types and people from different age groups and socioeconomic circumstances. Assess them, assess the emotions they have shown and your reaction to them.

- ❏ How often is there happiness in the people around you?

- ❏ How often is there sadness or anger in the people around you?

- ❏ How do these emotions make you feel?

- ❏ How long does it usually take you to pick up on their emotions? Do you need to talk a bit, do they need to tell you or do you see it as soon as they walk through the door?

- ❏ Do your emotions adapt to the emotions of those around you or do theirs adapt to yours?

- ❏ What is your reaction to the negative emotions of those around you?

- ❏ What is your reaction to the positive emotions of those around you?

- ❏ Who has the biggest influence on your emotions without any actual attempts from them?

WRITING PROMPT: EMPATHY

WRITING PROMPT: EMPATHY

HOW TO EMBRACE YOUR OWN NATURE

"In order to heal, it is essential to gather the strength to think negatively. Negative thinking is not a doleful, pessimistic view that masquerades as 'realism'. Rather, it is a willingness to consider what is not working. What is not in balance? What have I ignored? What is my body saying no to? Without these questions, the stresses responsible for our lack of balance will remain hidden." — Gabor Maté

We are all flawed, this is a fact of life. We try and be good people, we try and do the right thing, but we won't always succeed and that is okay. One of the most important ways of healing is to accept exactly who and what we are. When you have accepted yourself, flaws and all, they cannot be used against you anymore. When you know how valuable you are and how amazing you are, you cannot be told otherwise. But I think the most important thing is that, if you have already been broken down and made to hate yourself, when you start accepting who you are, you realize that your flaws are nowhere near as bad as you thought they were, and your good attributes are a lot better than you were made to believe.

You need to accept your entire nature, accept that you are high maintenance, accept that you are an empath, accept that you are a good painter, accept that you are a sloppy drunk. You should accept every aspect of yourself, no matter how good or how bad you think it is.

Embrace Your Own Nature

This is easy to say, but how do we actually implement this? Here are a few steps to help:

- **Step 1: Embrace yourself.** Look at the things that make you special. Look at all your values, personality traits and quirks. Make a list of all of them and then next to each one write down how it *adds* to your life. This should be purely positive additions, even when you address negative traits of yourself. For example, "Jealousy - This helps me to make sure that my partner makes time for me."

- **Step 2: Be compassionate to yourself.** Make a list of everything you have ever done wrong. It should be a long list because we all make mistakes in our daily lives. If the list feels too long, only write the ones down you feel the most guilty for. Next to each of them, write down your reasoning for it. Put your feelings aside, and for a moment ignore your guilt about this. Write what made you do this. Why did you do this? Then after each explanation write an affirmation, even if it's just, "I understand and it is okay."

- **Step 3: Reflect using your new knowledge.** Take a look back at your life, paying attention to the things you made a list of in the previous step. Have you done them again, and how do you feel about these actions now? Take a look at your past actions, emotions and feelings and reflect on how far you have come since then. If you feel at all that there are negative aspects to you that you have not grown from, remember that you are currently looking at them, and that in itself is growth.

- **Step 4: Identify and acknowledge your strengths.** By now you should already have a list of your good attributes; look at this list, expand on it every time you think of something new and when someone says something negative about you, look at this list, remind yourself about it and if you find something that you can use to shut them down, do it respectfully. Something along the lines of, "I understand you think I am not a good writer, but I have several published books and positive reviews to prove you wrong."

- **Step 5: Be happy for you.** You have achieved many things in your life, you achieve many things everyday, even if that thing is only waking up and getting out of bed. I understand that this is a cliché, but please realize that it is indeed true. This is the step where you have to start celebrating every achievement in your life. Have you gotten a compliment from a customer at work? Celebrate it! Have you completed a project recently? Celebrate it! Have you managed to stick with your budget this month? Celebrate it! Celebrate each and every achievement, even if you do it alone; when you have the opportunity, celebrate it with friends; if you complete a project at work, ask your friends to come over, have a barbecue or some drinks, have coffee if that is your thing, tell everyone the big news, let them congratulate you and be happy about it

Step 6: Forget the critic. Does Catherine Ann Cora or Gordon Ramsey care if a critic enters their restaurant, or is the critic scared of reviewing their restaurant? Personally I don't see anyone looking forward to writing any of these people a bad review, and I understand why. Now implement that same tactic on yourself. You know you are excellent. You demand perfection and you manage to deliver it. So that critic either has an ax to grind or is looking for their moment of fame. And our inner critic is looking for the latter. It wants to break you down and be the most important voice you ever hear. That is where CBT comes in. Recondition yourself, and when your inner critic pops up and says something negative, shut it down and know it is lying to you.

Step 7: Make some plans. Make a plan of how you can avoid the people that bring negativity into your life and challenge you on this journey. Make plans for how you will continuously rebuild and support yourself. Create re-affirmations, plan retreats, set a goal for a certain amount of outings you need to do per month. Just be sure that you plan for your own success.

Step 8: Move on. Ensure that you let go of the past, the things that were done to you and all your disappointments. Forgive, but do not forget. Always remember how you have been hurt; don't forget it and ensure you do not get back into that situation. As important as it is for you to change these situations, to change and to improve yourself, it is good to let go of the anger. If you do not let go of your anger, you will always focus on it, it will influence your emotions and it will dominate your thoughts. This will hold you back and continuously place you back into those situations.

Step 9: Build your support structure. Any bridge, any building, any structure needs supports, whether those supports are built into the foundations or hanging on the outside to keep it up, or both. You as a person are the same. If you feel that you cannot speak to those close to you then I would suggest that you find out from your local hospital or community center whether they have support groups, or maybe even find one you like online. The important thing is that you have a non-judgmental space where you can speak freely.

Step 10: Forget everything. Your journey is unique to you. Your thoughts and feelings are unique, so don't let anyone tell you what to do. I am trying to guide you and you will find others that do the same, but when someone tells you exactly what to do, and claims that there is only one way to go and that all other ways are ridiculous and wrong, they do not have your best interests at heart.

I would like for you to explore your own nature, to self-identify with and accept it. I would like you to get down all of you, each and every part that makes you, well, you. Look at where it came from and how it helped to form you.

WRITING PROMPT: NATURE

Writing Prompt: Nature

Journal Prompt: Create a Character

In this prompt I want you to create a book character, but this character should be you. I want you to write like how an author would write one of their characters. Describe yourself physically, describe your traits and give a background on them, describe the clothes you wear, the hobbies you have and any other part of yourself, and explain where it comes from.

CREATE A CHARACTER

FEELINGS AND DREAMS

It is an established fact that your dreams are your mind's way of processing your life. While we are awake, our mind stores our memories all jumbled and crazy, and then, when we go to sleep, all this stored information is sorted out, processed and the unimportant bits thrown away, while the important parts are filed away in proper locations so our brains can get to it easily when needed. This is what happens when we dream, and that is why dreams normally incorporate things that happened to us during the day, and things we tend to still try and process.

So why is it important that we look at this? To put it simply, this is your brain's—and by extension your inner self's—way of telling you what it is having trouble working through and processing.

So, when we do experience issues in our current everyday lives that connect back to previous issues from our past lives, our dreams are usually the first to indicate this to us. If we feel emotions that we are not always completely sure what they mean or why, our dreams can usually tell us why using the comparisons they make for us.

"The dream is the small hidden door in the deepest and most intimate sanctum of the soul, which opens to that primeval cosmic night that was soul long before there was a conscious ego and will be soul far beyond what a conscious ego could ever reach."
— Carl Gustav Jung

I want you to hold off this prompt and do it tomorrow morning as soon as you wake up. I want you to pay special attention to what happens to you during the day, and then to your dreams, and see how your brain processed the information.

- ☐ What are key aspects of your dream that stood out to you?

- ☐ What are aspects of your dream that seemed unimportant?

- ☐ Were there any people or referencing to people in your dream?

- ☐ When is the last time you saw these people?

- ☐ When is the last time you thought about these people?

- ☐ What aspects of your dream correlated directly to events that happened during the day?

- ☐ What aspects of your dream correlated to events that happened during the past month?

- ☐ What aspects of your dream correlated to events longer than a month ago?

- ☐ Why do you think the older events are still prevalent in your dreams?

- ☐ Were there any recurring aspects to your dreams?

- ☐ Was there any representation of fears, phobias or trauma in your dream?

- ☐ Did any of these fears or traumas present themselves to you in your life recently?

- ☐ What positive aspects were there to your dream?

- ☐ What negative aspects were there to your dream?

- ☐ Did you see any presentation of your Shadow Self in your dream?

WRITING PROMPT: DREAMS

WRITING PROMPT: DREAMS

Journal Prompt: Shadow Work and Daily Rituals

In this prompt I want you to take the entire book and everything you have learned into consideration. Then I would like you to think of the future. Write down what your daily rituals will be to help you heal; this can be things like making a list of boundaries you want to implement in your life once a month. This journal prompt should be your way of exploring how you can use these techniques in daily rituals to help improve your life.

CONCLUSION

We have now reached the end of the book, but our journey is not at an end. This is simply the part where you have grown and learned enough to spread your own wings.

Although I did not have the chance to personally meet you, I count myself lucky to have been part of your journey so far and I wish you the best moving forward. Remember that you are not bound to your past, and that you can become the person you truly want to be.

Your journey of self-discovery and healing has just begun, and hopefully this book has helped you with those first steps, so that you are now better equipped to look at your life on an ongoing basis. You can better deal with trauma both old and new.

Putting together this book has been just as much of a journey for me, and I have poured my heart and soul into it. This is why I am confident that you will be able to pour your heart and soul into the journey as well.

You have looked at your beginnings, what shaped you, what made you and what hurt you. You have learned how to deal with those wounds and to accept the parts of you that you may not always be proud of. But I think, more importantly, you have learned how not to let others use those parts to break you down and control you, and how to heal from where this has already happened.

If you feel the need to take this journey again, you can always just use a blank piece of paper and revisit the writing and journal prompts again, read the book again and restart your journey. You can also use what you have learned and adapt it to fit into your life going forward.

I also realize that there are aspects of this book that have likely been especially difficult. It is not easy setting boundaries and keeping with them, it is not easy cutting people from your life, and it is certainly not easy being completely honest when self-reflecting, but you have done it. So, take a moment and be proud of yourself.

I would like to leave you with a cliché—but remember, just because it's a cliché does not mean it's not true: You can do anything as long as you believe in yourself.

"Forgiveness of self is where all forgiveness starts." — Neale Donald Walsch

Thanks for being here

If you found value in this material, please consider leaving a short review, your testimonial would mean a lot to us and other readers.
To thank you for your purchase complete the following 2 steps and get your Bonuses!

Step 1: Leave your review

   Scan QR-Code

Step 2: Claim your additional audiobook "Guilt and Shame" **absolutely free!**

Scan QR-Code

AUTHOR BIO

You may have been wondering who is this Victoria Stevens person that has been giving me advice, and what makes her qualified to do so? I would like to take a moment and tell you more about myself.

I was born in 1973 in San Francisco, California. In this picturesque city, my life was a sharp contrast. My childhood was made dark by verbally abusive parents who gave me my own trauma at a young age. This decimated my confidence and self-image and led to me moving from one troubled environment to the next for the longest time.

Throughout this entire time, my brain was working, thinking, and wondering about how my adult life tied in with my childhood, and eventually, the obsession became enough to push my life into a new direction.

I started to delve into theories of developmental psychology and childhood trauma, which I found helped to alleviate my suffering and could be used to help those around me also alleviate their suffering.

Before I knew it, one thing had led to another, and today I am the author of several successful Self-Help books. I've helped thousands of people to heal the wounds they have been carrying around throughout their entire life. Together we have helped them to regain a healthy and successful self-image, we have healed their inner child and have integrated their Shadow Selves to help them achieve a new sense of wholeness and freedom. My daily practice has been heavily influenced by many renowned psychologists, psychotherapists, and physicians such as Carl Jung (which is why you'll see he is the main influence in this book as well).

Aside from that, I grew up in a household that was not very religious, so I also never became very religious myself, but still found myself loving nature and feeling connected to the outside world. One of the ways that helped me feel very connected was journaling about everything, and that got me thinking about how we could use this to by-pass the usual religious ideas behind self-improvement and healing.

I found that my passion for journaling makes a great alternative for meditation and other religiously influenced techniques. Journaling it helps me to record my thoughts and feelings, then reflect on them and plan forward, thinking of where I am going in life. This is an aspect of analytical psychology which I have become an avid enthusiast of throughout my career.

I decided that I want to use the skills and research that I have accumulated throughout the years to inspire others, as this will help me to make the most of my own values and furthering the research and knowledge will also help me to advance my career as a writer.

So, I made it my mission to share the most effective methods that I have found—such as the famous "Shadow Work Journaling Workbook", "CBT-inspired writing prompts" and "3 Letters to Improve Personal Awareness and Authenticity"—with as many people as I can.

When I am not working or writing, I retreat to my favorite place to self-reflect, the sea. I have found the ocean offers serenity, it offers a place for people to celebrate their joy and socialize with each other and to enjoy the unpredictable ocean. When I head out on the ocean with my sailboat, I feel at peace and connected with my inner self. This is when I truly allow the beauty of life to surprise me.

I hope that throughout this book you got to see my heart and vision beyond the ordinary, and that you will let it take you on a journey of growth and love while fighting your insecurities with me. If we can do this, I know this book will offer you a life-changing experience.

REFERENCES

10 ways to practice self-acceptance. (2018, June 19). Kids Help Phone. https://kidshelpphone.ca/get-info/10-ways-practice-self-acceptance/

American Psychological Association. (2017, July). *What is cognitive behavioral therapy?* American Psychological Association. https://www.apa.org/ptsd-guideline/patients-and-families/cognitive-behavioral

AMFM. (2019, November 25). *Trauma bonding: What is it and why do we do it?* A Mission for Michael. https://amfmtreatment.com/trauma-bonding-what-is-it-and-why-do-we-do-it/#:~:text=Trauma%20bonding%20occurs%20when%20a

Arends, K. (2020, March 16). *20 journaling prompts i swear by to get you out of your head.* Wit & Delight. https://witanddelight.com/2020/03/20-journaling-prompts-i-swear-by-to-get-you-out-of-your-head/#:~:text=Journaling%20Prompts%20for%20Self%2DDiscovery

Being, G. (2021, November 13). *7 stages of trauma bonding.* Grace Being. https://grace-being.com/narcissistic-abuse/7-stages-of-trauma-bonding/#stage-1-love-bombing

Brenner, G. H. (2018). *Attachment style, adult well-being, and childhood trauma.* Psychology Today. https://www.psychologytoday.com/us/blog/experimentations/201801/attachment-style-adult-well-being-and-childhood-trauma

Brown, M. (2022, March 31). *What radical acceptance is — and isn't.* Psych Central. https://psychcentral.com/blog/what-it-really-means-to-practice-radical-acceptance#definition

Cassata, C. (2021, September 25). *Flaws and all: how to accept yourself in 8 steps.* Psych Central. https://psychcentral.com/lib/ways-to-accept-yourself

C.G. Jung quotes. (n.d.-a). Goodreads. Retrieved August 25, 2022, from https://www.goodreads.com/author/quotes/38285.C_G_Jung?page=6

Cherry, K. (2020, August 2). *Is love biological or is it a cultural phenomenon?* Verywell Mind. https://www.verywellmind.com/what-is-love-2795343

Cherry, K. (2021a). *Cognitive behavioral therapy.* Verywell Mind. https://www.verywellmind.com/what-is-cognitive-behavior-therapy-2795747

Cherry, K. (2021b, July 13). *Why rational emotive behavior therapy was created.* Verywell Mind. https://www.verywellmind.com/rational-emotive-behavior-therapy-2796000

Coping mechanisms. (2018). Good Therapy Blog. https://www.goodtherapy.org/blog/psychpedia/coping-mechanisms

Cornish, M. A., & Wade, N. G. (2015). *A therapeutic model of self-forgiveness with intervention strategies for counselors.* Journal of Counseling & Development, 93(1), 96–104. https://doi.org/10.1002/j.1556-6676.2015.00185.x

Cuncic, A. (2021, May 26). *What is radical acceptance?* Verywell Mind. https://www.verywellmind.com/what-is-radical-acceptance-5120614

Cuncic, A. (2022, January 25). *What is multimodal therapy?* Verywell Mind. https://www.verywellmind.com/what-is-multimodal-therapy-5216156

Definition of LOVE. (2019). Merriam-Webster.com. https://www.merriam-webster.com/dictionary/love

Difference between child abuse and child neglect. (2015, February 11). Difference Between. https://www.differencebetween.com/difference-between-child-abuse-and-vs-child-neglect/

Ducharme, J. (2018, June 5). *How to tell if you're in a toxic relationship — and what to do about it.* Time. https://time.com/5274206/toxic-relationship-signs-help/

Emotion regulation. (n.d.). Psychology Today South Africa. Retrieved August 2, 2022, from https://www.psychologytoday.com/za/basics/emotion-regulation#:~:text=Emotion%20regulation%20is%20the%20ability

Erozkan, A. (2016). *The link between types of attachment and childhood trauma.* Universal Journal of Educational Research, 4(5), 1071–1079. https://doi.org/10.13189/ujer.2016.040517

Gabor Maté quotes. (n.d.-b). Goodreads. Retrieved August 21, 2022, from https://www.goodreads.com/author/quotes/4068613.Gabor_Mat_

Henriksen, I. O., Ranøyen, I., Indredavik, M. S., & Stenseng, F. (2017). *The role of self-esteem in the development of psychiatric problems: a three-year prospective study in a clinical sample of adolescents.* Child and Adolescent Psychiatry and Mental Health, 11(1). https://doi.org/10.1186/s13034-017-0207-y

Hochenberger, K. L. (2021, July 26). *Co-parenting with a narcissist: The impossible dream.* Psychology Today. https://www.psychologytoday.com/us/blog/love-in-the-age-narcissism/202107/co-parenting-narcissist-the-impossible-dream?fbclid=IwAR3KwH1wMgdj-zhD3bHuIQvG9IJFzR0w0thc2r7I4hsiU-zL5fN1UXL3unKE#:~:text=Co%2Dparenting%20is%20not%20an

How to really "let go". (2017, August 23). Ekhart Yoga. https://www.ekhartyoga.com/articles/wellbeing/how-to-really-let go#:~:text=In%20its%20basic%20form%20

Hoy, D. (2020, January 31). *5 long-term benefits of therapy.* David Hoy and Associates. https://davidhoy.com/5-long-term-benefits-of-therapy/

Leonard, J. (2019, October 21). *Cognitive dissonance: Definition, effects, and examples.* Medical News Today. https://www.medicalnewstoday.com/articles/326738#:~:text=Cognitive%20dissonance%20is%20a%20theory

223 affirmations to heal from trauma and toxic relationships. (2022, March 12). LifeNGoal. https://lifengoal.com/affirmations-for-trauma-and-toxic-relationships/

Lindberg, S. (2020, October 23). *Benefits of therapy for yourself, family, and relationships.* Healthline. https://www.healthline.com/health/benefits-of-therapy#family

Linehan, M. M. (2015). *DBT Skills Training Manual.* Guilford Publications.

Marti, D. (2018, April 2). *How emotions enter our dreams and impact our health.* Diane Marti. https://wbplincoln.org/how-emotions-enter-our-dreams-and-impact-our-health/#:~:text=In%20essence%2C%20researchers%20discovered%20that

Mate, G. (n.d.-a). *Addiction expert, speaker and best-selling author Dr. Gabor Maté.* Dr. Gabor Maté. Retrieved August 25, 2022, from https://drgabormate.com/

Maté, G., & Levine, P. (2010). *In the realm of hungry ghosts : close encounters with addiction.* North Atlantic Books, Lyons, Colorado.

McBride, K. (2012, May 7). *It's all about me: recovery for adult children of a narcissist.* Psychology Today United Kingdom. https://www.psychologytoday.com/gb/blog/the-legacy-distorted-love/201205/it-s-all-about-me-recovery-adult-children-narcissist

Monroe, H. (n.d.). *Video Teachings.* Monroe Wellness. Retrieved August 21, 2022, from https://www.monroewellness.com/video-teachings

Narcissistic personality disorder - symptoms and causes. (2017, November 18). Mayo Clinic. https://www.mayoclinic.org/diseases-conditions/narcissistic-personality-disord er/symptoms-causes/syc-20366662#:~:text=Narcissistic%20personality%20disorder%20%E2%80%94%20one%20of

Neale Donald Walsch quotes. (n.d.-b). Goodreads. Retrieved August 25, 2022, from https://www.goodreads.com/author/quotes/9374.Neale_Donald_Walsch?page 5

Newport Academy. (2017, September 1). *How relational trauma impacts teen mental health, social connections, and self-esteem.* Newport Academy. https://www.newportacademy.com/resources/mental-health/relational-trauma/#:~:text=Relational%20trauma%20occurs%20when%20there

Patrick Patrick Carnes. (2019). *Betrayal bond: Breaking free of exploitive relationships.* Health Communications, Incorporated.

Phoenix | mythological bird. (2018). Encyclopœdia Britannica. https://www.britannica.com/topic/phoenix-mythological-bird

Preventing adverse childhood experiences. (2020, September 3). CDC. https://www.cdc.gov/violenceprevention/aces/fastfact.html#:~:text=Adverse%0childhood%20experiences%2C%20or%20ACEs

Ramani Durvasula quotes. (n.d.-c). Goodreads. Retrieved August 25, 2022, from https://www.goodreads.com/author/quotes/5813517.Ramani_Durvasula?page 2

Raypole, C. (2021, May 17). *Ready, set, journal! 64 journaling prompts for self-discovery.* Psych Central. https://psychcentral.com/blog/ready-set-journal-64-journaling-prompts-for-self-discovery

Sarkis, S. A. (2022, June 20). *The 3 stages of a toxic relationship.* Psychology Today. https://www.psychologytoday.com/us/blog/here-there-and-everywhere/202206/the-3-stages-toxic-relationship

Scarpelli, S., Bartolacci, C., D'Atri, A., Gorgoni, M., & De Gennaro, L. (2019). *The functional role of dreaming in emotional processes.* Frontiers in Psychology, 10. https://doi.org/10.3389/fpsyg.2019.00459

Starecheski, L. (2019). *NPR choice page.* NPR. https://www.npr.org/sections/health-shots/2015/03/02/387007941/take-the-ace-quiz-and-learn-what-it-does-and-doesnt-mean

76 healing c-ptsd quotes and affirmations + free printable flashcards. (n.d.) The Wellness Society. Retrieved August 21, 2022, from https://thewellnesssociety.org/76-healing-cptsd-quotes-and-affirmations/

Vaknin, S. (2015). *Malignant self-love: Narcissism revisited.* Narcissus Publications.

Van Der Kolk, B. (2014). *The body keeps the score: Brain, mind, and body in the healing of trauma.* Penguin Books.

Walker, P. (n.d.). *Pete Walker, M.A. psychotherapy*. Pete Walker. Retrieved August 25, 2022, from http://www.pete-walker.com/

Weber, M. (2021, February). *How attachment styles affect adult relationships*. Help Guide. https://www.helpguide.org/articles/relationships-communication/attachment-and-adult-relationships.htm

What is love? (2017, March 6). Good Therapy Blog.   https://www.goodthera-py.org/blog/psychpedia/love

What are ACEs? And how do they relate to toxic stress? (2019). Center on the Developing Child at Harvard University.   https://developingchild.harvard.edu/resources/aces-and-toxic-stress-frequently   asked-questions/

Wooll, M. (2022, June 13). *8 benefits of shadow work and how to start practicing it*. BetterUp. https://www.betterup.com/blog/shadow-work

Zambon, V. (2020, October 30). *What is an empath?* Medical News Today. https://www.medicalnewstoday.com/articles/what-is-an-empath#signs

IMAGES

Andrews, A. (2017, June 27). *Broken black flip phone* [Image]. Unsplash. https://unsplash.com/photos/bxhYCD7cdq8

Ardivan, M. (2021, June 9). *Photo by Marcel Ardivan on Unsplash* [Image]. Unsplash. https://unsplash.com/photos/E20mDo9QEAc

Barrett, T. (2017, September 9). *Silhouette of people* [Image]. Unsplash. https://unsplash.com/photos/hvvRg72aXCw

Barros, J. A. (2018, July 31). *Silhouette of road signage during golden hour* [Image]. Unsplash. https://unsplash.com/photos/C7B-ExXpOIE

Bazzocco, M. (2019). *Don't forget to live signage photo* [Photograph]. Unsplash. https://unsplash.com/photos/nvnZnE1eDLQ

Beamer, D. (2019). *You didn't come this far to only come this far lighted text photo* [Photograph]. Unsplash. https://unsplash.com/photos/Vc1pJfvoQvY

Burden, A. (2016, September 6). *Swing chair hanged outdoor* [Image]. Unsplash. https://unsplash.com/photos/_p5CoeXeF_I

Cleveland, G. (2015). *Dandelions with motivational quote on board* [Photograph]. Pixabay. https://pixabay.com/illustrations/word-art-dandelion-saying-quote-859057/

Espinoza, M. (2021). *Quote motivation lettering* [Photograph]. Pixabay. https://pixabay.com/illustrations/quote-motivation-lettering-art-6704983/

Fadi Xd. (2018, August 30). *Close-up photography of heart shaped fairy lite on brown sand* [Image]. Unsplash. https://unsplash.com/photos/I4dR572y7l0

Ferrario, A. (2019, June 17). *Brown clouds* [Image]. Unsplash. https://unsplash.com/photos/3WgPZbsDSkE

Grimstad, H. (2020, September 20). *Photo by Håkon Grimstad on Unsplash* [Image]. Unsplash. https://unsplash.com/photos/hteXWSF9jA4

Mossholder, T. (2017). *you are worthy of love sign beside tree and road* [Photograph]. Unsplash. https://unsplash.com/photos/SR8ByN6xY3k

Motoc, A. (2020, January 26). *Person holding clear glass heart shaped pendant* [Image]. Unsplash.com; Unsplash. https://unsplash.com/photos/qxHiV5nIOjc

Nik. (2018). *difficult roads lead to beautiful destination desk decor photo* [Photograph]. Unsplash. https://unsplash.com/photos/z1d-LP8sjuI

Planeta, L. (2016). *Self esteem motivation positivity* [Photograph]. Pixabay. https://pixabay.com/photos/self-esteem-motivation-positivity-5603700/

Ravat, A. (2022). *Motivation quote inspiration* [Photograph]. Pixabay. https://pixabay.com/illustrations/motivation-quote-inspiration-cutout-6959764/

Singh, Y. (2017a, November). *Shallow focus photography of person holding a lighter* [Image]. Unsplash. https://unsplash.com/photos/pHj23cFO1hg

Singh, Y. (2017b, November). *Shallow focus photography of person holding a lighter* [Image]. Unsplash. https://unsplash.com/photos/pHj23cFO1hg

StockSnap. (2017). *Still items things* [Photograph]. In Pixabay. https://pixabay.com/photos/still-items-things-book-notebook-2607434/

Vessey, J. (2017, September 12). *Woman standing on sands near shoreline* [Image]. Unsplash. https://unsplash.com/photos/W7VYL56u2sc

Wood, J. (2016). *Motivational quote* [Photograph]. Pixabay. https://pixabay.com/photos/accomplish-quote-motivation-1136863/